P9-DOA-014

HIKING & BIKING IN LAKE COUNTY, ILLINOIS

by Jim Hochgesang

Cover photography by Glenn Jahnke
Design by Melanie Lawson
Edited by Sheryl DeVore

A Roots & Wings Publication

ORLAND PARK PUBLIC LIBRARY

917.7321
HOC

11/03 3/03
LAD
TU 12

© Copyright 1994 by Roots and Wings,
Lake Forest, Illinois
Second Printing, 1996

All Rights Reserved. Reproduction of any part of this
guidebook without written permission is prohibited.

Created by Sandy and Jim Hochgesang
Design by Melanie Lawson
Offset printing service by Rheitone, Inc.
Printed and bound by United Graphics, Inc.

Roots and Wings assumes no responsibility or liability for
accidents or injuries by people using this book to explore
the hiking and bicycling trails described.

ISBN 1-884721-00-1

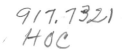 Printed on Recyled Paper.

ORLAND PARK PUBLIC LIBRARY

3 1315 00217 8734

HIKING &
BIKING IN
LAKE COUNTY,
ILLINOIS

Contents

Acknowledgments

We appreciate the support, input, and guidance of many professionals who reviewed our draft manuscript, provided source maps, and supplied information.

> Steve Barg, Walter E. Heller Interpretive Center and Nature Park
> Marty Buehler, Lake County Department of Transportation
> John Dempsey, Village of Buffalo Grove
> Ruby Holmquist, Illinois Trailriders
> Jim LaBelle, North Point Marina
> Ken Leone, Lake Forest Park Department
> Greg Malin, Village of Vernon Hills
> Stacy Miller, Volo Bog State Natural Area
> Betsy Otto, Chicago Openlands Project
> Bob Pushee, Zion Park District
> Ed Rodiek, Chain O'Lakes State Park
> Sarah Surroz, Mike Fenelon, and Diana Dretske, Lake County
>   Forest Preserve District
> Susan Wright, Illinois Beach State Park
> Sheri Ziemann and Jeff Austin, Chicago Botanic Garden

The maps included are derived from source maps provided courtesy of Lake County Forest Preserves, Illinois Department of Conservation, Heller Interpretive Center, Illinois Trailriders, the City of Zion, and the City of Highland Park.

A special thanks to the women and men involved in developing and maintaining the trails and pathways in Lake and the adjoining counties.

Preface

He sidearms the flat stone onto the surface of the spring rain swollen Des Plaines River. One-two-three skips. Our seven year-old son, Jeffrey, smiles with a new achievement. Fast forward three months. On a warm summer day four hawks soar effortlessly above Gander Mountain nestled in the far northwestern corner of Lake County. Their view is even better than that of the humans who discover them while enjoying the panoramic scene of Lake and McHenry Counties spread below. Fast forward three months. The fallen oak and maple leaves scratch their backs as the wind blows them along the crushed gravel path on the Des Plaines River Trail chasing the bikers that they will never catch. Fast forward three months. Six inches of newly fallen snow welcome the family of cross country skiers as they glide down the trail in Ryerson Woods. The only sound comes from their skis swishing through the snow.

Our family moved to Lake County in the fall of 1983. We soon discovered cross country skiing on the forest preserve trails near our home. The spring, summer, and fall brought opportunities to trek through the woods and prairies while enjoying beautiful wildflowers, song birds, and the peaceful serenity. My wife and I love to take long walks and ride bikes. Due to convenience and our lack of knowledge of what was available, we tended at first to repeatedly visit the same spots. We found, from talking to friends and acquaintances, as well as to people we met on the trails, that many others followed the same routine.

Over time, we ventured farther and discovered many interesting new pathways in Lake County that were still relatively close to home. Thus, the idea for this guidebook was born.

Lake County, Illinois, offers many unique forests, parks, and trails available for hikers and bikers all year. The purpose of this guide is to provide helpful information on available sites and how to find them. We've also included a little history of the area. Some 230 miles of trails and pathways are described. Exploring 30 different sites and talking with the people responsible for creating and maintaining them was great fun. We hope you enjoy the trails as much as we do. Happy hiking and biking!

Introduction

Many of us today spend our working hours sitting at a desk or in front of a computer or machine inside office, factory, or store. Statistics indicate we are working longer hours and that job stress is increasing due to corporate downsizing and the drive for productivity propelled by domestic and international competition.

At home, when we pick up a newspaper or turn on the television, we are deluged with news about community, national, or international tragedies or crises. Family and financial pressures only add to this matrix of stress.

Physical exercise provides an excellent and positive way to relax and release the stress. And there is no better way to get physical exercise than in a natural setting while walking, hiking, biking, cross country skiing, horseback riding, or engaging in other outdoor activities. You're out there breathing the fresh air, soaking up nature, and forgetting the concerns and problems that often clutter your mind.

While it is most convenient to leave the front

Lake County Forest Preserves

A family hike on the Des Plaines River Trail.

door and embark on one of these activities in your neighborhood, why not consider the nearby parks and preserves? Drive or better yet bicycle to a forest preserve. Spend an hour, a half day, or a full day walking, biking, and picnicking. You'll find the woods, lakes, rivers, prairies, and savannas to be relaxing, peaceful environments where you can put things into perspective. Being in a forest and observing nature can even help lower your heart rate and blood pressure.

Through the remarkable process of photosynthesis, trees and other plants take in carbon dioxide that humans have expelled and combine it with water and sun to create food. The byproduct is oxygen for us to breathe.

Forests cool us in summer and reduce wind and noise. In forests, too, we can observe the ultimate in recycling as dead leaves and plant material decompose adding nutrients to the soil. Plant roots also act as anchors to help prevent water runoff.

Lake County, Illinois, is blessed with some of the most beautiful natural areas in the Midwest. This guide describes the many trails that wind through the county's natural environment. These are perfect spots for hiking and biking. They vary in difficulty and length offering opportunities for those of all ages with different skill levels. Running, cross country skiing, canoeing, picnicking, and other outdoor activities can also be enjoyed in the county's parks and preserves.

A Lake County map, identifying the listed parks, forests, and trails is included on pages 20 and 21. Following the map, you'll find a summary table listing information on each site.

More detailed information follows in the descriptions of 30 preserves, parks, forests, and trails that provide opportunities for hiking and off-road bicycling in Lake County. Each section tells you how to get to the site, where to park, what facilities are available, and trail lengths. Also included are individual trail maps and special information about plants and animals that can be seen at the sites as well as education centers, a museum, and other attractions for you to visit. Where appropriate, proximity to the Metra train line is identified. For example, Forest Park Beach is a pleasant 1 mile walk from the Metra North Line train station in Lake Forest.

The Lake County Forest Preserves are open from 8 a.m. to sunset every day, except for Ryerson Conservation Area which is only open until 5 p.m.

The guide is organized in geographical sections somewhat like a sideways "S" starting with the Green Bay Trail in the southeastern section of the county and heading north along or close to Lake Michigan to Kenosha, Wisconsin, on the North Shore Path. Heading west, the Des Plaines River lies 6 to 8 miles inland. The river roughly parallels the Lake Michigan shoreline and is surrounded by Lake County forest preserves as it flows to the Cook County border. Many of the preserves as well as community bikeways and other trails interconnect with the Des Plaines River Trail or will in the near future.

In western Lake County, the preserves and parks are mostly islands with little interconnection today. We'll head back north ending at Gander Mountain in the far northwestern tip of the county.

Following the trail and preserve descriptions is a look to the future. There is a growing interest in establishing more trails for hiking and biking and interconnecting the existing pathways. Some of the plans to establish new greenways are discussed.

Hiking

Questions hikers often ask are: What if I don't want to take a long hike? Where can I take a short walk with my five-year-old? Where can I find a path that continues for more than just a few miles?

Lake County has walks and hikes to meet all your needs. Distances vary from less than 1 mile to 20 miles or more round trip. You can take your young children on a short walk less than 1 mile at Ryerson Conservation Area where a bench to sit down and look over the Des Plaines River can be found halfway. Or you can embark on round trip hikes of 20 miles or more on the northern and southern sections of the Des Plaines River Trail by venturing into the preserves and side paths along the trail. Soon the two sections will be interconnected to provide even longer adventures.

Biking

Every cyclist blazes his or her own trails from once around the block to across the country. We could fill this book writing about and showing maps of bike trails throughout Lake County involving routes on public roads and highways that are often used. But we won't do that. An objective of this guide is to make you aware of Lake County parks, forests, and dedicated off-road trails for walking, hiking, and biking. Many of the parks and forests described in this guide provide multi-use trails including biking. You can use your bike instead of your car to get to the preserve or park. Bike racks are available in most locations. You save gas and get more exercise. We'll touch on a few bike routes on highways and public roads but only to provide inter-connection from one preserve or dedicated trail to another.

Rules of the Trail

With the growing number of multi-use trails, you may encounter bicyclists, runners, wheelchair users, hikers, equestrians, rollerbladers, and others on the pathway. Please be courteous and considerate of others so that everyone can enjoy our Lake County trails. Safety suggestions and regulations to protect the environment are described following this introduction. Please read this section now. If you do not thoroughly read and comply, all the air will be let out of your bike's tires and/or your hiking boots will squeak!

More Information On Programs

The Lake County Forest Preserves offer nature programs and activities year-round. The organization also publishes a free newsletter *Horizons*. Call 708-367-6640. Several of the other agencies that manage the sites described in this guide also offer programs and activities, publish newsletters, provide detailed trail maps or guides, or have more information available about a particular site. Telephone numbers are included.

Nearby Attractions, Calendar of Events, Organizations

In the appendices, you will find a listing of attractions and merchants furnished by the Lake County Convention and Visitor's Bureau. A Calendar of Events includes many annual Lake County activities by month. You will also find a listing of environmental, hiking, bicycling, and other related organizations. Additional information has been provided by a few merchants and agencies.

While we worked to find as many appropriate events and organization listings as we could, certainly through oversight or ignorance, we missed some. Please notify us of any oversight for future issues of this guidebook. Our address is Roots & Wings, P. O. Box 167, Lake Forest, Illinois 60045.

Comments/Order Form

To improve future issues of *Hiking & Biking in Lake County*, your comments would be very much appreciated. A comments form is included on page 127. We'd also like to know if you'd be interested in future hiking/biking guides. Page 128 contains an order form if you'd like to purchase additional copies of this book for your friends and family.

The trails and pathways of Lake County are there for your use. Enjoy!

Rules of the Trail

- Deposit litter in proper receptacles.
- Leave nature as you find it for others to enjoy.
- Leash all pets. (Some preserves do not allow pets.)
- Remain on the trail.
- Be alert for cars or bicycles.
- Don't feed the wildlife.
- Lake County forest preserves are open 8 a.m. to sunset daily. Hours of operation for other sites are shown in the sections describing each site.
- Don't wear earphones. You can't hear a bicyclist coming.
- Relax, have fun, and enjoy!
- Check for ticks when you're finished.

Specific for Bicyclists

- Wear a helmet.
- Be alert for loose gravel, debris, holes, or bumps on the trails.
- Take it easy with hikers of all ages on the trail.
- Ride in single file.
- Cautiously pass hikers on the left. Call out "passing on the left". But remember the hiker may be deaf or hard of hearing or may be wearing earphones.
- Keep both hands on your handle bars.
- See "Illinois Bicycle Rules" for additional safety information for on-road bicycling.

For your enjoyment

- Apply insect repellent before you go out dependent on the season.
- Take water on long hikes or bike rides.

A Little History

Five hundred million years ago Lake County, Illinois, was buried beneath a vast ocean, the Silurian Sea. Extinct marine animals including trilobites and cephalopods as well as graceful sea lilies lived, died, and formed the limestone that today supports much of the Midwest. At the Lake County Museum in Lakewood Forest Preserve, you can see a remnant of these ancient times—a 420 million-year-old fossil rock embedded with shellfish, sea lily, and coral.

For 50 million years, the Silurian Sea evaporated and shrunk to what is today the Gulf of Mexico while hills, arches, and great valleys formed in the Midwest. Huge lush forests of fern-like trees grew, died, and decomposed first into peat and millions of years later into coal. The Michigan Basin, a deep depression, was also created and would later become Lake Michigan and Lake Huron. Over time, through erosion, endless flats of sand and clay were created.

Then, beginning about one million years ago, during the Pleistocene glacial epoch or Ice Age, four separate movements of massive ice slowly moved southward pushing stone and rock and sculpting the land. The last two glacial movements, the Illinoisan and the Wisconsonian, carved out the Lake Michigan basin, leaving behind a fertile black topsoil that would later attract a flood of settlers to farm the fruitful Lake County prairies.

As the glaciers melted, water runoff created smaller lakes, rivers, and streams such as Chain O'Lakes and the Des Plaines and Fox Rivers. Lush prairies and savannas teeming with grasses and wildflowers as well as forests comprised of oak, maple, pine, and other trees evolved and flourished.

First Inhabitants

Approximately 35,000 years ago, humans crossed the Siberian land bridge into North America for the first time. By 11,000 B. C., their descendants, the Paleo Indians, had migrated to the Midwest. The now extinct mastodon as well as deer, buffalo, elk, wolf, fox, squirrel, muskrat, and beaver thrived. Flocks of pigeon, geese, ducks, and cranes filled the sky. These animals as well as copious plant life provided sustenance for the Paleo Indians.

Even as recent as 300 years ago, Lake County resembled a giant preserve of forests, wetlands, and prairies. Some 5,000 Algonquin Indians, mostly of the Potawatami tribe, lived then in what is now Lake County. They hunted, fished, and planted maize, working to be part of the natural environment and striving to live in harmony with it.

White man's interest in the territory was stimulated in 1673 when Jacques Marquette, a Jesuit priest, and his companion, Louis Joliet, canoed the Des Plaines River and explored Lake Michigan's shoreline. In 1833, the Potawatami ceded control of what is now Lake County to the rapidly expanding United States government. The first white settler, Captain Daniel Wright, built a cabin near the Des Plaines River banks in 1834 near what is today Riverwoods. At the same time farther north, Amos Bennett, the first African American settler in the area, built a cabin along the Des Plaines River near what is now Gurnee. Other settlers quickly moved in as the Indians moved out. Land could be bought at $1.25 per acre then and settlers eagerly cleared prairies, savannas, and forests to raise corn and wheat. Lake County grew quickly as settlers learned how productive the northern Illinois soils were. Prairies were plowed under to feed not only the area residents, but also the burgeoning population in Chicago where corn and wheat grown in Lake County were transported.

Sewage and other debris were deposited into the Des Plaines and Fox Rivers, which flowed onto the topsoil and tilled lands. By 1940, industrial development had sprung up in Lake County, particularly near Waukegan and North Chicago. Industrial waste was conveniently dumped into the area rivers as well as Lake Michigan.

We have all in some way disturbed the ecology of Lake County. We litter streets, roads, rivers, and lakes. We use fertilizers and pesticides that pollute rivers and lakes.

A Wonderful Place for Hiking and Biking

Area residents became concerned about how human practices have harmed Lake County, one of the most attractive areas in the Midwest with its Lake Michigan shoreline, many wetlands, forests, and prairies. The need to restore, protect, and sustain has now become a priority. Concerned citizens, businesses, and government officials are working to reverse the damage done. Through recycling efforts, improved industrial and solid waste and sewage disposal, and non-polluting land practices, real progress is being made.

A critical enabling force is the Lake County Forest Preserve District which owns 85 percent of the land bordering the Des Plaines River in Lake County as well as many other preserves. Its mission is "to preserve a dynamic and unique system of diverse natural and cultural resources, and to develop innovative educational, recreational, and cultural opportunities of regional value, while exercising environmental and fiscal responsibility." Prairies and savannas are being restored. New wildlife habitats are being established.

A major effort has been underway to improve, maintain, and develop hiking and biking trails to provide recreational opportunities in a natural setting. In addition to the Lake County Forest Preserves, the Illinois Department of Conservation, the Lake County Department of Transportation, community parks departments, and other organizations are involved in developing paths and trails.

As you hike and bike the wetlands, prairies, and forests along Lake County's extensive trailway system, please do your part to preserve, protect, and restore our natural environment.

Lake County Forest Preserves, Trails, and Parks

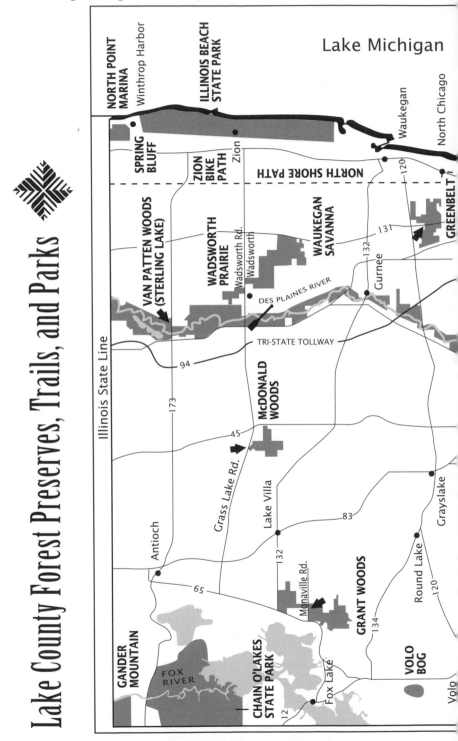

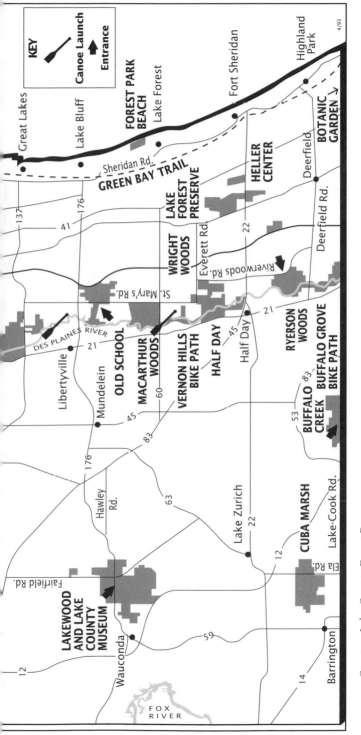

Courtesy Lake County Forest Preserves

Lake County, Illinois Hiking and Biking Trails

Park Preserve or Trail	Book Section	Miles of Trails Hike	Miles of Trails Bike	Author's Comments
Green Bay Trail	1	18.0	18.0	Asphalt/crushed gravel trail from Wilmette to Lake Bluff.
Heller Nature Park	2	3.3	—	Bike rack available. Wood chip and gravel trails.
Forest Park Beach	3	1.0	—	Bike racks available. Long boardwalk down the bluff and brick path along the beach.
Lake Forest Preserve	4	2.0	—	Undeveloped dirt trails. No parking access. Need to walk or bike to site.
North Shore Bike Path Heading North	5	15.4	15.4	Crushed gravel surface, from North Chicago to Kenosha, Wisconsin. Connects with Pike Trail in Wisconsin for additional 9.3 miles north to Racine.
Heading West		5.5*	5.5*	From Lake Bluff train station to Mundelein. Trail construction planned between I-94 and Libertyville. Planned to connect with DPRT.
Zion Bike Path	6	6.3	6.3	Crushed gravel and asphalt surface. Planned to connect to Illinois Beach State Park trail system.
Illinois Beach State Park South Unit	7	5.0*	—	Mixture of gravel, wood chip, and sand surfaces. A new 5.5 mile multi-use trail is planned to extend north to Spring Bluff Forest Preserve.
North Unit		6.7*	6.7*	Planned to connect with Zion Bike Path.
North Point Marina and Spring Bluff Forest Preserve	8	on road bed only*		North of Illinois Beach State Park. Undeveloped trails in Spring Bluff.

Park Preserve or Trail	Book Section	Miles of Trails Hike	Bike	Author's Comments
Des Plaines River Trail (DPRT)** Northern Section	9	9.0*	9.0*	Planned to run from Wisconsin border to Cook County. Crushed gravel surface. Open to equestrians. Planned to connect with Southern Section.
Van Patten Woods and Sterling Lake Forest Preserve		7.0	6.0	5 miles open to equestrians.
Greenbelt Forest Preserve	10	5.0	4.0	Crushed gravel trails.
Des Plaines River Trail (DPRT)** Southern Section	11	8.8*	8.8*	Planned to extend to Cook County Forest Preserve Trail. DPRT open to equestrians.
Old School Forest Preserve		6.0	5.5	3.5 miles open to equestrians.
Wright Woods Forest Preserve		5.0	4.5	4.5 miles open to equestrians.
Half Day Forest Preserve		2.0	2.0	1 mile open to equestrians.
Vernon Hills Bikeways	12	7.0*	7.0*	Asphalt and concrete 8-foot wide surface. Interconnects with DPRT. Planned to interconnect with North Shore Path–west, and Buffalo Grove bike path system.

Park Preserve or Trail	Book Section	Miles of Trails Hike	Bike	Author's Comments
Ryerson Woods Conservation Area	13	6.5*	—	Wood chip, grass, and dirt trails. Self-guided nature trails, environmental trails, environmental education center.
Chicago Botanic Garden	14	17	2.0	Connects via sidewalk to Green Bay Trail. Off-road path planned. Northern trailhead for North Branch Bicycle Trail.
North Branch Bicycle Trail	14	17.3	17.3	Mostly asphalt. From Chicago Botanic Garden to Devon Avenue in Chicago.
Buffalo Grove Bike Path System	15	32.9*	32.9*	8-foot wide asphalt and concrete bike path. Planned to interconnect with DPRT at Ryerson, Vernon Hills Bike Path, Buffalo Creek Forest Preserve, and Wheeling Bike Path.
Buffalo Creek Forest Preserve	16	4.0*	4.0*	Crushed gravel trail currently under construction. Will connect with Buffalo Grove Bike Path System. Completion 9/94.
Cuba Marsh Forest Preserve	17	4.0	—	Mown grass trails. No parking area. Need to park along Cuba Road.
Lakewood Forest Preserve	18	9.0	—	6.5 miles open to equestrians. Trails are not suitable for biking.
Volo Bog State Natural Area	19	3.3	—	.5 mile boardwalk nature trail through the bog and 2.8 miles Tamarack Trail.
Grant Woods Forest Preserve	20	3.3	3.3	Crushed gravel trail.

Park Preserve or Trail	Book Section	Miles of Trails		Author's Comments
		Hike	Bike	
McDonald Woods Forest Preserve	21	3.0	2.0	2 miles of crushed gravel trail. 1 mile of wood chip and grass trail.
Chain O'Lakes State Park	22	15.8*	5.0*	8 miles of dirt trails open to equestrians and hikers, 5 miles of crushed gravel hiking and biking trails, and 2.8 miles of nature trails.
Gander Mountain Forest Preserve	23	2.5	—	Undeveloped trails. Highest elevation in Lake County.

*Signifies additional trails under construction or planned.

**Des Plaines River Trail traverses many Lake County forest preserves. The Northern Section runs through: Van Patten Woods/Sterling Lake, Wadsworth Savanna, Wetlands Demonstration Area, and Gurnee Woods. The Southern Section passes through: Old School, MacArthur Woods, Wright Woods, and Half Day. Additional trails off the DPRT are available at some of those preserves as shown.

Reader's Comments

Green Bay Trail

In the early 19th century, travelers used an old Indian ridge trail to make the trip from Fort Dearborn in Chicago to Fort Howard in Green Bay, Wisconsin. On foot the trip took one month. The present Green Bay Trail is a lot shorter— approximately 18 miles from Shorewood Park in Wilmette in Cook County to Lake Bluff. Built on the right of way of the departed Chicago North Shore Milwaukee Railway, the Green Bay Trail parallels the Metra North Line (C & NW) railroad tracks as well as Greenbay and Sheridan Roads.

How to get there:

Ample parking along the trail is available. Since this is a Lake County guide we'll describe locations near the north trailhead and south county border. The Ravinia Festival Park south lot on St. John's Avenue in Highland Park just north of Lake Cook/County Line Road is a good choice. But don't leave your car there after 4 p.m. in the summer when Ravinia concerts are in session or you'll get a parking ticket. You can also park in Turnbull Cook County Forest Preserve just south of Lake Cook Road on Green Bay Road, although this requires riding or walking north along busy Green Bay Road for .15 mile. Head right (east)

The Green Bay Trail in Highland Park.

.2 mile to the Braeside train station. At the north end of the Green
Bay Trail, park in downtown Lake Bluff anywhere near the train
station where the trail entrance is located.

The 7-mile Cook County portion of the trail heading north from
Shorewood Park takes you through Wilmette, Kenilworth, Winnetka,
and Glencoe. The trail winds through a series of parks: Shorewood,
Sheldon, and Veteran's Memorial. Water and restrooms are easily
available. The surface is asphalt for the first few miles with some
street crossings. In Kenilworth near the train station, watch for the
"bike route" signs. We saw practically no litter or glass on the path.
For most of its length in Cook County, the trail closely parallels the
Metra railroad tracks with few street crossings. As you enter Glencoe
the surface changes to packed gravel. The path is mostly a dedicated
off-road trail except for the interludes at each community's train
station where you'll need to use the street or parking lot. The dedicated trail begins again at the far end of the train station parking area.

The Green Bay Trail enters Lake County in Highland Park at the
Braeside train station just south of Ravinia at Lake Cook/County Line

Green Bay Trail

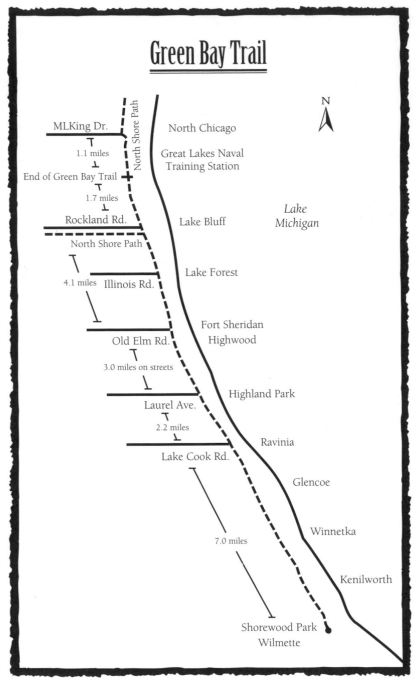

N

MLKing Dr.

North Chicago

1.1 miles

Great Lakes Naval
Training Station

End of Green Bay Trail

1.7 miles

Rockland Rd.

Lake Bluff

*Lake
Michigan*

North Shore Path

Lake Forest

4.1 miles Illinois Rd.

Old Elm Rd.

Fort Sheridan
Highwood

3.0 miles on streets

Laurel Ave.

Highland Park

2.2 miles

Lake Cook Rd.

Ravinia

Glencoe

7.0 miles

Winnetka

Kenilworth

Shorewood Park
Wilmette

Road. Heading north into Lake County, the surface is crushed gravel. About 1 mile north of Lake Cook, you'll come to the Ravinia train station. You'll find restaurants nearby across the railroad tracks. For a short side trip, head east on Roger Williams Avenue past Jens Jensen Park. After .75 mile, you'll come to Rosewood Beach Park where a scenic view amidst the trees on a high bluff overlooking Lake Michigan awaits you. A bike rack is available. Nearby is a stone stairway winding its way through the trees down to the beach. A very pretty spot! You'll then need to backtrack to the train station to continue north on the Green Bay Trail. The off-road trail temporarily ends at the downtown Highland Park train station at the intersection of St. John's and Laurel Avenues. Good places for food and drink are in the Port Clinton area on Central Avenue. Bike racks are available.

To continue north take St. John's to Central Avenue. Turn right (east) to Sheridan Road. Turn left (north) on Sheridan. Three quarters of a mile from Central Avenue you'll pass Moraine Park. You may want to stop here for drinking water, restrooms, picnic areas, and a lovely view of Lake Michigan. Follow the signs for Sheridan Road north into Highwood by way of Edgecliff Drive, Oak Street, and Walker Avenue.

Fort Sheridan, the recently closed United States Army base is on your right. Hopefully, a portion of this area will become a forest preserve with trails through the deep woods and along the bluffs overlooking Lake Michigan. Continue north along Sheridan Road using the sidewalk that runs in front of the former army base property. After traveling 3 miles through Highland Park and Highwood, you'll come to the Fort Sheridan train station at the intersection of Old Elm Road and Sheridan Road north of Highwood. The dedicated bike trail starts up again here north of the train station parking lot. The asphalt pathway is sandwiched between the Metra train track on the left and Sheridan Road on the right. In late 1993, this part of the trail up to downtown Lake Forest was totally resurfaced. As you travel north into Lake Forest, you'll pass Barat College. Then you'll see South Park with ball fields and a playground area for the kids. You'll have only one street crossing between Old Elm and downtown Lake Forest. This portion of the trail ends in downtown Lake Forest at Illinois and McKinley Roads. Be careful going down the short but steep decline.

Take McKinley north. In 1994, two bridges will be constructed to improve the trail. The first bridge will cross over Illinois Road to the train station parking lot.

Downtown Lake Forest offers several good restaurants. At the first stop sign at Deerpath and McKinley, you have three pleasant alternatives—1) Turn left across the track at the train station and explore the Market Square area. This was the first shopping center in the country (built in 1916). 2) Turn right on Deerpath Road and ride 1 mile to Forest Park with scenic bluff views of Lake Michigan. You'll find bike racks by the stairs to the beach. A long elevated boardwalk winds its way through the trees to the shoreline. You can also take a short hike on the brick walkway along the Lake Michigan beach. (See Section 3 for a description of Forest Park Beach). 3) To continue on the dedicated bike path proceed straight on McKinley for 4 blocks north of the train station to Woodland Road. The asphalt bike path resumes on the northwest corner of Woodland and McKinley. In 1994, a bridge will be constructed over Woodland from the north end of the train station parking lot to the off-road Green Bay Trail.

From downtown Lake Forest you have a 1.7 mile ride to downtown Lake Bluff. On the way you'll pass Lake Forest High School, a beautiful Georgian style building that you may remember from the movie "Ordinary People." There are two Y intersections on the trail right before you go over the bridge to the Lake Bluff train station. Proceed straight ahead at the Lake Bluff train station to continue north on the Green Bay Trail. Either of the two paths to the left take you to a bikeway paralleling Route 176 heading west. This is the west branch of the North Shore Path. (See Section 5 for the North Shore Path.)

There is a asphalt surface for 1.7 miles north of the train station to the city limits. The Green Bay Trail ends there and the North Shore Path starts. The surface is concrete as you enter North Chicago for 1.1 miles. To your right is the Great Lakes Naval Training Center. If you want to continue north, see Section 5 for interconnection to the north branch of the North Shore Path in downtown North Chicago. I think there is a law of grammar that says one cannot use the word "north" four times in one sentence. Please forgive us!

Walter E. Heller Interpretive Center and Nature Park

The Park District of Highland Park operates this 97-acre forest and nature center on the far north side of the community.

How to get there:

The entrance is on the east side of Ridge Road which is just west of and parallels Route 41. The park is south of Old Elm Road and north of Route 22.

You'll discover 3.3 miles of woodchip or crushed gravel trails for walking or cross country skiing in the winter. This is a good place to bring young hikers because the trails range from .3 to 1.5 miles. On your visit you may see "Sky", the resident red-tailed hawk, on the arm of one of the Heller staff. You will pass through a canopied pine forest on the Red Trail and can observe the power of nature where a 1991 tornado cut a swath of destruction through the forest. The Blue Trail takes you through a mixed hardwood forest to a small pond. A prairie flourishes near the interpretive center. Trails are open from dawn to dusk.

A Discovery Room is fun to explore for children of all ages. Many school groups also visit the center during the school year. A picnic

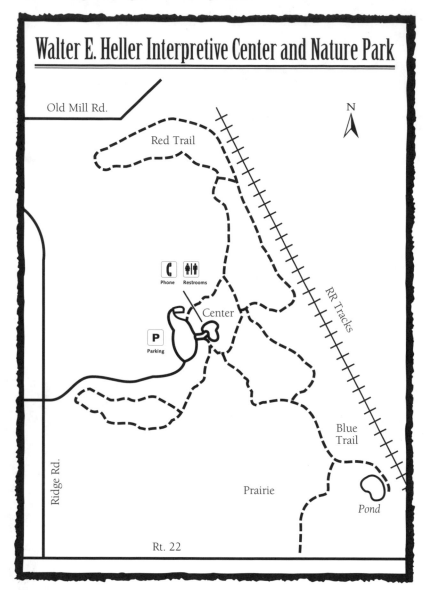

Walter E. Heller Interpretive Center and Nature Park

area, restrooms, drinking water, and telephone are available. This educational facility offers many nature and environmental programs. Cross country skis are available for rent in winter. Call 708-433-6901 for more information.

Forest Park Beach

Forest Park sits on a bluff in east Lake Forest overlooking Lake Michigan. In May 1987, the community of Lake Forest re-opened the beach after a major and successful shoreline restoration and construction project. Forest Park Beach is a beautiful place to walk and watch the sailboats lazily floating on the lake. A long wooden board-walk zigzags through the woods from the top of the bluff to the beach below. Be sure to take this walkway if you hike down to the beach. Along the beach a wide brickwalk with park benches every few feet winds its way for over half a mile. A con-cession stand (in the summer), swimming, rest-room facilities, and drinking water are available

How to get there:

Take Deerpath Road 1 mile east of downtown Lake Forest. Parking at Forest Park Beach is for residents with a city parking permit only. Out-of- town visitors can bike from the Green Bay Trail (see Section 1) or walk 1 mile from down-town Lake Forest. Bike racks are available at Forest Park. Or you may want to take the Metra North Line train. Free parking is available on Forest Avenue, off of Deer-path 2 blocks west of Western Avenue.

Lake Forest Preserve

Lake Forest Preserve on the west side of Lake Forest has about 2 miles of undeveloped trails.

How to get there:

The entrance is on Old Mill Road .8 mile north on Waukegan Road from Half Day Road (Route 22). Turn right (east) onto Old Mill Road. Proceed .4 mile until the auto road ends. No parking is available, so you'll need to hike or bike to the preserve. You could also bicycle here from the Heller Interpretive Center (Section 2) taking Ridge Road north to Old Mill; then west to the auto barricade. Walk or bike over the Skokie River bridge to the entrance.

Follow the asphalt pathway straight ahead past the auto barricade. An undeveloped dirt path to the south leads into an old estate property. After about .2 mile you'll come to a small lake encircled by a dirt path. To the east, paths lead first through a deep woods and then through a large open meadow. No facilities are available here and the trail is not maintained other than an occasional mowing, so wear long pants. No formal trails are planned here, but this is a quiet, peaceful area where you can hear birds singing and see many butterflies dancing through the meadow.

North Shore Bike Path

The North Shore Path (NSP) runs north from Lake Bluff to the Wisconsin border at Russell Road near Winthrop Harbor and west from Lake Bluff to Mundelein. Today the trail interconnects with the Kenosha County Bicycle Trail, the Green Bay Trail, and the Zion Bike Path. Interconnection with the Des Plaines River Trail and with the Illinois Beach State Park trail system via the Zion pathway are planned for 1994. As a result, the NSP is becoming a major arterial route providing transport to many communities, parks, and forest preserves in eastern Lake County.

Heading West

The Green Bay Trail described in Section 1 runs north to Lake Bluff. There it interconnects with the two branches of the North Shore Path. One heads west, the other north to Wisconsin. The path to the left just before crossing over the bridge on Rockland Road (Route 176) at the train station in Lake Bluff is the start of the west leg of the NSP. There are now 5.5 miles of a completed bike path with more planned. The asphalt trail heads west along Rockland Road. First follow Carter Avenue and then Thornwood Lane until the off-road trail resumes at the intersection of Thornwood and Sunset Roads. The beginning portion of the trail is hilly and windy in spots so stay to your right and go slowly. At Green Bay Road an .8-mile asphalt bike trail heads north past the Lake Bluff community pool and golf course. This northbound path ends at the Lake Bluff city limits. You'll need to backtrack to the North Shore Path. In the fall of 1993, the NSP was extended to Lambs Farm at Route 176 and I-94. Cross over Waukegan Road at the light and continue on the new crushed gravel trail. On the left (south) is a forest and to the right a business/industrial area. New bridges have been added which elevate the NSP over working railroad tracks.

Lambs Farm is a non-profit training center for the mentally handicapped. Festivals and many special events are held year-round. You may enjoy the children's farmyard, miniature golf, ice cream parlour, bakery nook, country store, and restaurant.

Farther west 2.4 miles of the path is open from 4th Avenue in Libertyville just east of Milwaukee Avenue (Route 21) to Brice Avenue in Mundelein. Just west of Butterfield Road is Marytown/St. Maximilian Kolbe Shrine, operated by the Franciscan Friars. You can visit the historic shrine, walk the beautiful grounds and browse through the gift shop. (See page 118 for more information.) I suggest crossing Route 176 at the stoplight at Carmel High School.

Plans exist to extend the NSP west from Lambs Farm to 4th Avenue and to interconnect with the Des Plaines River Trail near Rockland Road. When completed, the western section of the bike path will run over 7 miles from Lake Bluff to Mundelein. Completion is planned for 1994-1995.

Heading North

Back at the Lake Bluff train station the northbound asphalt path will take you into Wisconsin. The Green Bay Trail picks up again just north of the train station. Note the scenic open pasture area on the right as you leave downtown Lake Bluff. In the summer, the trees form a canopy to shade the walkers, bikers, and runners. The Green Bay Trail ends at the northern border of Lake Bluff where it interconnects with the NSP. Continue north on the concrete sidewalk to North Chicago.

North Shore Bike Path

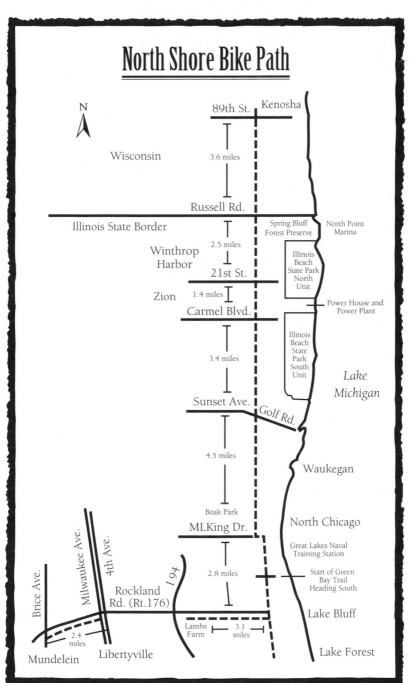

N

89th St. — Kenosha

Wisconsin

3.6 miles

Russell Rd.

Illinois State Border — Spring Bluff Forest Preserve — North Point Marina

2.5 miles

Winthrop Harbor

Illinois Beach State Park North Unit

21st St.

Zion   1.4 miles

Carmel Blvd.

Power House and Power Plant

Illinois Beach State Park South Unit

3.4 miles

Lake Michigan

Sunset Ave.

Golf Rd.

4.5 miles

Waukegan

Boak Park

North Chicago

MLKing Dr.

Great Lakes Naval Training Station

Milwaukee Ave.

4th Ave.

I 94

2.8 miles

Start of Green Bay Trail Heading South

Brice Ave.

Rockland Rd. (Rt.176)

Lake Bluff

Lambs Farm   3.1 miles

2.4 miles

Mundelein   Libertyville

Lake Forest

You'll notice to your right the Great Lakes Naval Training Station, which trains 30,000 recruits annually. The base covers 1,628 acres and employs over 9,000 military and 3,500 civilian employees. The number of recruits and employees will be increased substantially in the near future due to the closing of other naval bases. The off-road NSP temporarily ends at Martin Luther King Drive in North Chicago.

How to get there:

Parking is available at many places along the path. At the southeast trailhead, park in Lake Bluff near the train station (see Section 1 for connection to Green Bay Trail). At the north trailhead in Kenosha, park along 89th Street near Anderson Park at the intersection with 30th Avenue. Parking is available on the streets of the communities you pass through (Winthrop Harbor, Zion, Beach Park, Waukegan, and North Chicago). You'll see signs identifying the location of the North Shore Path. The trail is just east of and parallel to Lewis Avenue from North Chicago to the Wisconsin state line.

If you are biking or hiking north from downtown North Chicago, turn left (west) across the train tracks on Martin Luther King Drive 2 blocks to Commonwealth Avenue. Turn right (north) on Commonwealth following the "Bike Path" signs. The off-road NSP picks up again at Boak Park 1 block north of Broadway Avenue.

The NSP is built on the old North Shore Railway Line right-of-way and runs straight through northeastern Lake County and then interconnects with the Kenosha County trail in southeastern Wisconsin. From Boak Park in North Chicago to Kenosha the bike path runs 15.4 miles, 11.8 in Illinois, and 3.6 in Wisconsin. The crushed gravel path proceeds through the urban communities of first North Chicago and then Waukegan. There are 17 street crossings between Broadway Avenue and Yorkhouse Road (4.1 miles of the path).

With the street congestion, this portion may not be suitable for families with young children. If you don't want to ride through the urban areas of North Chicago and Waukegan, start on the north side of Waukegan at Golf Road. Take Route 41 to Delaney Road north to Sunset Avenue. Head right (east) on Sunset which becomes Golf Road. Then turn right (south) at the bike path sign on to Western Avenue.

Park your car on one of the side streets near the Lake County YMCA. From Golf Road you'll find 10.9 miles of trail to the outskirts of Kenosha. You'll encounter only three street crossings over 3.4 miles until you enter the town of Zion. Here the trail becomes part of the Zion Park District Bike Path for 1.4 miles. The surface is asphalt in Zion with eleven street crossings.

Just north of 21st Street in Zion the crushed gravel path resumes at a trail intersection. Take the trail left. The city of Zion bike path continues to the right (see Section 6). The setting changes from an urban to a rural environment with woods and meadows on both sides. The North Shore Path is well maintained, although you may encounter broken glass in some spots, particularly in or near the urban areas.

As you cross the state border at the Russell Road overpass, the path is labeled the Kenosha County Bike Trail. It continues north for 3.6 miles and is even more bucolic and rural than the Lake County section. The dedicated trail ends on the outskirts of Kenosha at 89th Street. Stop for a rest across the street at Anderson Park. You'll find restaurants 1 mile north on 30th Avenue at 80th Street. If you're ready for more miles, the city of Kenosha's Pike Trail continues north and interconnects with another bike path heading 9.3 miles north to Racine. The first part is through the streets of Kenosha. It becomes an off-road trail again north of town.

Heading back south from 89th Street in Kenosha is 21.8 miles round trip if you park near the Waukegan YMCA mentioned above or 37.2 miles round trip back to the Lake Bluff train station. Adding on all or part of the western portion of the NSP, the Zion Bike Path, and the Green Bay Trail, with the backtracking involved can easily double that distance. Translation: Bring your water bottle! Restrooms, water, and food are available at restaurants in the communities along the way but there are some long stretches without facilities.

In the near future, extensions of and the connections to the Illinois Beach State Park trail system, the Des Plaines River Trail, as well as the Vernon Hills and Buffalo Grove Bikeways, will be completed. Coupled with the North Shore Path, Zion Bike Path, and the Green Bay Trail, eastern and south central Lake County will have an excellent interconnected trail system.

Zion Bike Path

The Zion Park District has a 6.3-mile loop path with an asphalt surface. Four miles of the trail is an off-road bikeway while 2.3 miles is on the street. A segment of the trail serves as part of the North Shore Path (see Section 5). Plans are underway to interconnect with the Illinois Beach State Park trail system in 1994.

How to get there:

Take Sheridan Road (Route 173) to Zion. Parking is available throughout the community. The western portion of the trail, which serves as part of the North Shore Path, runs along Galilee Avenue from Carmel Boulevard on the southwest to 17th Street on the northwest. Here the North Shore Path splits left. To stay on the Zion Bike Path take the asphalt trail right. At the top of the hill follow the "bike path" sign right (east) on Ravine Drive. The bike route continues on the street for a short distance through a residential neighborhood until the intersection at 18th and Gideon Streets. The off-road asphalt path resumes here on the left and enters Beulah Park

Zion Park District Bike Trail

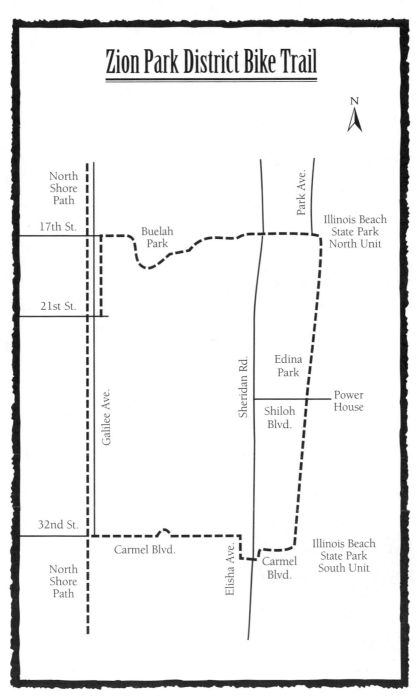

Nature Area. The trail winds its way through a forest with a long wooden bridge over a creek. This area is a bit hilly and curvy but very pretty and quiet.

The off-road path ends at 17th Street with a fairly steep hill to climb. At the time of writing, there were no bike signs here. Continue on the street east for a couple of blocks to Sheridan Road. This is a busy highway so be very careful crossing the street. You'll find restaurants south on Sheridan Road. Continue east on 17th Street to Park Avenue. The off-road Zion Bike Path picks up again just past Park on the right heading south. Farther east on 17th is the Northern Unit/Camp Logan area of Illinois Beach State Park (see Section 7) if you want to extend your ride.

Assuming you stay on the Zion Bike Path, continue south through the woods. The trail passes through Edina Park where you can enjoy a small lake and many ducks. On the last Sunday in April 4,000 runners gather here for the start of the Lake County Races. (See page 118 for more information.) After you leave the park, the path re-enters the woods for a distance. At Shiloh Boulevard, you can head east to Lake Michigan for a visit to the Power House (see page 117 for more information). Interconnection is planned here in 1994 between the Zion pathway and the Illinois Beach State Park trail system. The bike path then curves west and comes to a stop at Sheridan Road and Carmel Boulevard. Ride to the left along Sheridan for a half block to 33rd Street. Cross over Sheridan and head right (west) 1 block to Elisha Avenue. Again turn right on Elisha 1 block to 32nd Street. Continue west several blocks through residential neighborhoods until the street ends temporarily at Sharon Park. Head right for a short distance to an asphalt path that heads down a small ravine and crosses over a wooden bridge. Follow the trail back to 32nd Street and continue west. Soon you'll cross over Galilee Avenue which completes the 6.3-mile loop.

Call the Zion Park District at 708-746-5500 for more information.

Illinois Beach State Park

More than two million visitors each year come to Illinois Beach State Park. Many lay on the beach and venture into the chilly waters of Lake Michigan during the summer vacation season. But there is much more to the park. Spread over 4,160 acres and 6.5 miles of shoreline are picnic and camping areas, a nature center, and 12 miles of trails through woods and dunes. Some of the state's rarest wildflowers and other plant life grow here.

How to get there:
South Unit

The main entrance is on Wadsworth Road just south of Zion and north of Waukegan. Take Green Bay Road (Route 131) or Sheridan Road (Route 173) to Wadsworth Road. Head east to the main entrance. Follow the signs to the nature preserve 1.2 miles from the railroad tracks.

There are 5 miles of trails in the south unit. All four trails described below originate from the nature preserve parking area. All are limited to hiking only to help preserve the native vegetation. Here you'll find the only remaining natural dunes in Illinois.

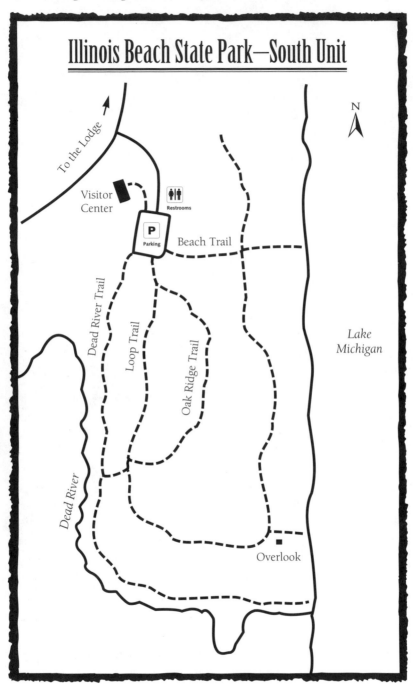

Illinois Beach State Park—South Unit

The Loop Trail is 2.3 miles of crushed gravel. You'll begin at a black oak forest which evolves into a sand prairie as you approach the beach. Stop at the 20-foot observation platform. This is the best view in the park with the Dead River entering into Lake Michigan to your right and the sand dunes and ridges rolling westward from the beach. On one visit, a killdeer played tag with us on the path; but it really was no contest since this common Illinois shorebird had the advantage of flight.

The Zion nuclear generator, the main source of electricity for the Chicago Metro area, is situated just north of the beach. Next to the sand dunes it appears out of place, and as a result Illinois Beach provides a stark portrayal of the contrast between the natural environment we inherited and the impact modern man has had on that environment.

The Beach Trail is a short .2 mile that starts on a wood chip pathway through the oak forest, then crosses a marsh over a long wooden bridge. As you enter the sand prairie and approach the beach you have just traveled through a good example of succession of plant life in a very short distance. On the beach no vegetation exists due to the harsh conditions caused by the waves and wind. In the sand prairie, hardy grasses start to grow. The wetland marsh is filled with cattails. Farther from the beach, black oak trees flourish.

The Oak Ridge Trail is a .6-mile half circle connecting with the Loop Trail. Appreciably cooler in the summer than the other trails due to the cover of the tall black oak trees, the trail is also a bit more hilly due to the ridges.

The 1.1-mile Dead River Trail starts at the southwest corner of the parking area and ends at Lake Michigan, paralleling the river for most of the way. The Dead River gets its name from the sandbar that forms across its mouth and stops it from draining into Lake Michigan. A nonmoving river is a "dead river"; hence, its name. When the Dead River backs up enough, it forces its way through the sandbar and empties into Lake Michigan. Along this trail, you can enjoy abundant wildflowers in spring and especially in late summer and fall such as milkweeds, shooting stars, and several kinds of gentians. You can also stop at a platform for a view overlooking the river and marshlands. If you're lucky, you might spot a green-backed heron fishing in the river.

The interpretive center in the nature preserve has exhibits and is open from 1 to 4 p.m. Friday through Sunday or by appointment. Restrooms and drinking water are available. A camp store near the beach in the South Unit is open in the summer with food, drinks, souvenirs, and public telephones. Cross country skiing is available in winter in both the North Unit and South Unit but not in the nature preserve. A lodge on the beach near the nature preserve is currently being renovated and will re-open in 1995.

A 5.5-mile multi-use trail is planned for construction in 1994 to run north from Old Beach Road near the nature preserve up through Camp Logan in the North Unit and on to the North Point Marina. Also, inter-connection with the Zion Park District Bike Path will provide easy access to the North Shore Path.

North Unit

The Camp Logan area in the North Unit contains a 6.7-mile Marsh Trail heading east out to the beach and north to the Spring Bluff Forest Preserve.

How to get there:

You'll find two access roads into the North Unit. In Zion, take 17th Street east off of Sheridan and park at Sand Pond or at the end of the road in the Dunes Day Use Area.

Farther north is another entrance. Take 7th Street east off of Sheridan Road in Winthrop Harbor to the North Point Marina Area. (See Section 8 for Spring Bluff Forest Preserve and North Point Marina). Turn right at the Harbor Administration Building. Take the next road right to the parking lot. From there a gravel road leads to the trail system.

The Marsh Trail is a mown grass surface through marshland, prairie, and lightly wooded areas. The trail leads to the beach in several spots. In some areas, particularly near North Point Marina, the trail is sandy so you may have to walk your bike. Around the Sand Pond, the trail surface is more compact and makes for easier biking. That area has more trees and is a nice place to hike. The new multi-use trail mentioned above will cut through this area and offer a very nice bike ride or long hike.

Illinois Beach State Park—North Unit

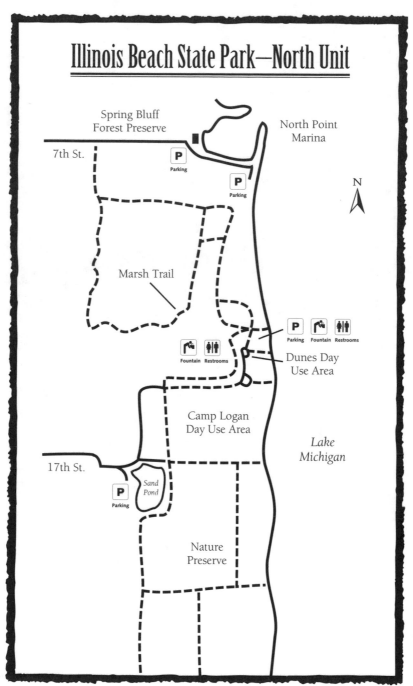

Glenn Jahnke

Duneslands at Illinois Beach State Park.

These trails are open to bicyclists, hikers, and cross country skiers in winter. Many programs and activities are offered year-round at Illinois Beach State Park. Call 708-662-4811 or 4828 for more information.

North Point Marina and Spring Bluff Forest Preserve

The Spring Bluff Forest Preserve, the state's largest marina, and the far northern part of Illinois Beach State Park are located just south of the Wisconsin border near Winthrop Harbor.

How to get there:

Take Sheridan Road (Route 173) to Winthrop Harbor then turn east on 7th Street. Continue toward Lake Michigan. You will pass the Spring Bluff Forest Preserve on your left (more on the preserve in a moment). You will then enter the North Point Marina area with 1,500 boat slips. The administration building is straight ahead just after a stop sign. You can park in the lot to the immediate right. A deli and coffee shop are nearby. For more information on the marina call 708-746-2845.

The Illinois Beach State Park beach area is right (south) of the marina. You may enjoy this beach area due to the smaller crowds, attractive marina, and the nearby Illinois dedicated nature preserve, Spring Bluff. Parking is on the right next to the beach. Note that most of the earlier parking lots are private for boat owners. Restrooms are located at the marina.

Spring Bluff is a 274-acre glimpse into how the land looked before the early settlers arrived. Owned and managed by the Lake County Forest Preserves, it has recently been included as part of the Illinois Nature Preserve System to further protect its rare wetlands and prairies. Special care of the land by users is urged.

The preserve provides habitat to many rare and state-endangered birds including American bitterns, Henslow's sparrows, upland sandpipers, and Virginia rails. While trails are not maintained, you can walk on an old roadbed through the preserve. Take the marina road to the far north end and park in the gravel lot.

A new 5.5-mile multi-use trail is planned for construction in 1994. Starting on 7th Street in Winthrop Harbor, the path will lead to the North Point Marina area near the administration building then head south through the Illinois Beach State Park North Unit (see Section 7).

With the planned Illinois Beach trail system hookup to the Zion Bike Path and from there to the North Shore Path and Green Bay Trail, the eastern part of Lake County will have an excellent interconnected trail system from the northern to the southern county border.

Des Plaines River Trail (DPRT) Northern Section

The Des Plaines River originates in Wisconsin. After meandering a bit in the northern part of Lake County, the river heads due south as straight as any river can into and through the western suburbs of Cook County. Then after a brief visit through the southeastern tip of DuPage County at the Argonne National Laboratory, the Des Plaines flows southwest through Will County near Joliet and on into Grundy County. There the Des Plaines meets the Kankakee River and together they form the Illinois River which then flows southwest. The Illinois River, in turn, is consumed by the Mississippi just north of St. Louis.

Protection of the Des Plaines River valley has been a priority for the Lake County Forest Preserve District since it was formed in 1958. In northern Lake County, the Des Plaines meanders through the wetlands, prairies, and savannas of the river valley. Farther south it mostly flows through woods and forests. A Lake County Forest Preserve, Van Patten Woods, surrounds the Des Plaines as soon as it crosses the state border. This embrace continues throughout most of the county. Eight-five percent of the land (nearly 6,500 acres) bordering the river in Lake

ORLAND PARK PUBLIC LIBRARY

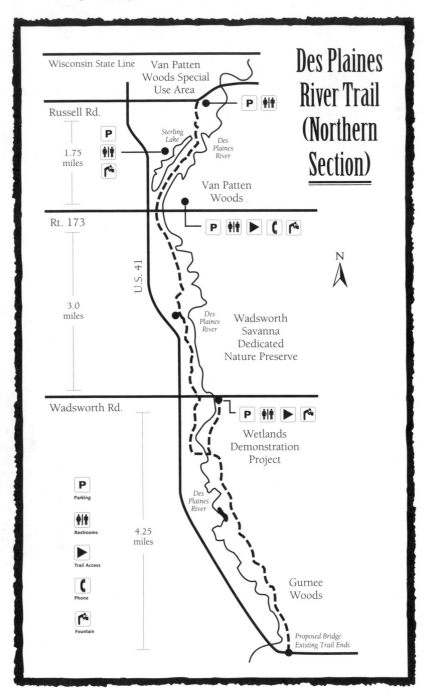

Wisconsin State Line   Van Patten
Woods Special
Use Area

P **[restrooms]**

Russell Rd.

P

Sterling
Lake

*Des
Plaines
River*

1.75
miles

[restrooms]

[fountain]

Van Patten
Woods

Rt. 173

P **[restrooms]** **▶** **C** **[fountain]**

U.S. 41

N

3.0
miles

*Des
Plaines
River*

Wadsworth
Savanna
Dedicated
Nature Preserve

Wadsworth Rd.

P **[restrooms]** **▶** **[fountain]**

Wetlands
Demonstration
Project

P
Parking

*Des
Plaines
River*

[restrooms]
Restrooms

4.25
miles

▶
Trail Access

C
Phone

Gurnee
Woods

[fountain]
Fountain

*Proposed Bridge
Existing Trail Ends*

Des Plaines
River Trail
(Northern
Section)

County is part of the Forest Preserves.

In 1981, an 8-mile multi-use trail paralleling the river was opened in the northern part of the county with an additional mile of trail added in 1989. In the fall of 1992, an 8.75-mile southern section opened. As funds are available, an additional 15 miles of trail will be added to span the county from Wisconsin to the Cook County border.

How to get there—Northern Section:

The northern trailhead starts at Russell Road just south of the Wisconsin border. Take U.S. Route 41 north to Russell Road. Turn right and continue on Russell Road for 1 mile. Park in the area for cars, and not in the horse trailer parking section. Restrooms, picnic tables, and drinking water are available. There is additional parking farther south near Sterling Lake just north of Route 173 and east of U. S. Route 41.

North of Russell Road is a special use area of Van Patten Woods. Recently a model airplane field has been added in a large open meadow. Also campgrounds are available for reservation by scouts and other youth groups. The road into the special use area consists of large gravel so go slowly if you bike there. It is worth the short trip to a very scenic view to the east and south.

The DPRT heads south from Russell Road. Follow the arrows on wooden markers to make sure you stay on the trail. (In some of the forest preserves there are several side trails available off the DPRT) The first preserve you enter as you start south is Van Patten Woods/-Sterling Lake.

Van Patten Woods/Sterling Lake

This beautiful 972-acre preserve offers picnic sites, play equipment for the children, play fields, a 5-mile bridle trail, and 7 miles of hiking trails. One trail winds its way around Sterling Lake with a bridge crossing over the water. In winter, snowmobiling (3 miles) and cross country ski trails (7 miles) are available. Shelters can be reserved for private parties. Drinking water and restroom facilities are also available. The angler will enjoy the shoreline fishing for blue gill, bass, walleye, muskie, and channel catfish at 74-acre Sterling Lake.

Van Patten Woods/Sterling Lake

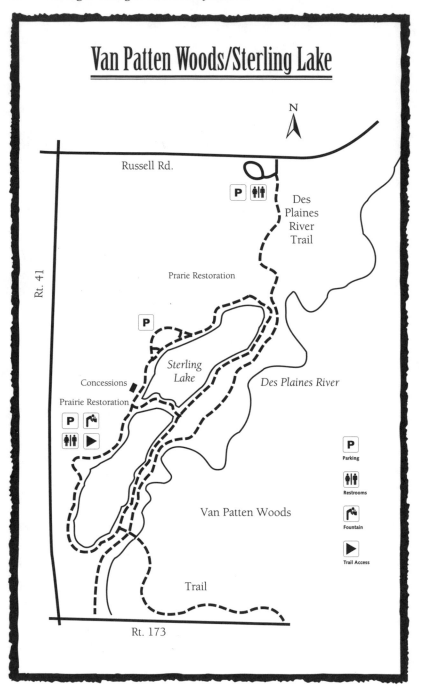

Biking at Sterling Lake.

Chandler's Boat and Bait Shop located right on the lake (708-526-8217) offers boat and bicycle rental, bait, tackle, snacks, and sundries.

This preserve is a good example of the restoration work done by the forest preserve district. This land was mined for gravel for 40 years until the mid-1970s. What is now beautiful Sterling Lake was once a big gravel pit. Restoration of the area has been underway for several years and was completed in fall of 1993.

Wadsworth Savanna

Continuing south on the DPRT, there is a highway crossing at Route 173 as you leave the Van Patten Woods area and enter into the Wadsworth Savanna. A portion of this 1,200-acre preserve is recognized as an Illinois Nature Preserve. A savanna is on the continuum between a prairie and a forest. Ecologists determine the difference by the amount of ground shaded by tree at noon. Prairies have up to 10% canopy cover, forests more than 80%, and savannas have a range of 10-80%.

Once tallgrass savanna was the dominate ecosystem in the upper Midwest supporting a tremendous variety of plants and animals. Elks,

The Wetlands Demonstration Area.

passenger pigeons, wild turkey, grouse, many varieties of butterflies, bluebirds, and hummingbirds abounded. Early settlers found these savannas to be excellent fields for their crops because of the deep, fertile soil. As a result, they were practically eliminated. In this area the DPRT winds mostly through open rolling hills with an occasional oak grove.

Wetlands Demonstration Project Area

After crossing Wadsworth Road (4.75 miles from the start at Russell Road), you enter the LCFPD's 550-acre Des Plaines River Wetlands Demonstration Project Area. This project provides large scale research for wetland construction and management. Rare species such as the endangered yellow-headed blackbird now nest here. In the spring, the entire area is often heavily flooded. Wetlands like these provide for water storage during floods and thus lessen damage downstream. Wetland vegetation also reduces erosion, helps to control pollution, and provides a home for various wildlife. The Illinois Department of Conservation estimates the state has lost 95% of its wetlands. Almost eight million acres have been converted to farmland.

You'll find a canoe launch just east of the DPRT as well as a short side trail out into the wetlands. As you continue south, you will cross a bridge over the river. Take a short side trip off the DPRT on the trail to the left which heads back north to the canoe launch. An observation platform there has a great view of the river bottom area in the spring. In summer, the view is blocked by the plants and trees. Also, a boardwalk along the river is a good place to either fish or just sit and watch the river go by. On my first hike through this area, I came upon a beaver who swam straight towards me, wiggled his nose, and then dove underwater.

Restrooms, drinking water, and parking are available at the canoe launch site on Wadsworth Road just east of U. S. Route 41.

South of the wetlands demonstration area the trail becomes rougher. Since this is all river bottom land, the flooding in the spring causes some washouts. Also the trail is used for horseback riding. But don't let that stop you. I ride a 10-year-old Schwinn touring bike and have had no trouble. Just be sure to take your time. The DPRT continues 4.25 miles south of Wadsworth Road. You'll pass by a lake and then mostly through wooded areas. The trail currently ends just north of U. S. Route 41 in Gurnee Woods.

Good news! Starting in the summer of 1994 the trail south of the wetlands area will be improved. A bridge will be constructed over U. S. Route 41 and the DPRT will be extended 1 mile south to Old Grand Avenue. A parking area will be built at Kilbourne Road. This will be a good addition to the DPRT establishing a convenient southern trailhead in Gurnee.

Greenbelt Forest Preserve

Located west of North Chicago and Waukegan, Greenbelt has 5 miles of hiking and biking trails through prairies, and marshland, and around two ponds.

How to get there:

Take Green Bay Road (Route 131) south of Belvidere Road (Route 120). The 559-acre preserve is divided into two sections by Green Bay Road. To enter the eastern side take Green Bay Road .5 mile south of Route 120 to 10th Street. Head east .7 mile on 10th till you reach Dugdale Road. Turn right (south) on Dugdale. The entrance will be on your right. The western side entrance is on Green Bay .8 mile south of Route 120.

The eastern section has a 1.5-mile marsh path and a .75-mile lake path looping around the pond. A 17-station fitness trail was getting a lot of use on my hike. Gently rolling hills, a variety of wildflowers, and some oak groves provide a peaceful island near the urban environment of Waukegan.

The western side mirrors the eastern with a 1.3-mile marsh trail and a .7-mile lake trail. All

Greenbelt Forest Preserve

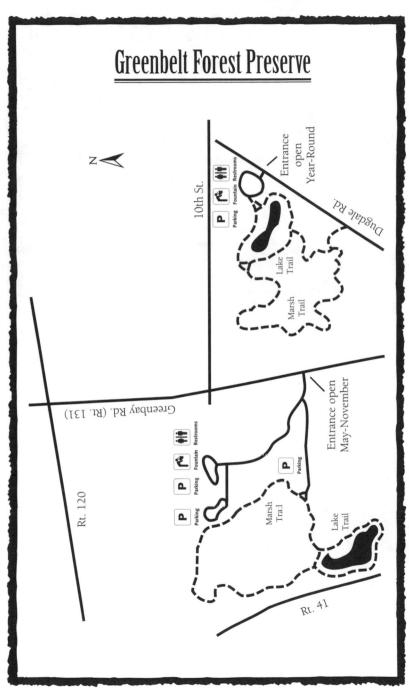

Lake County Forest Preserves

On the trail at Greenbelt Forest Preserve.

the trails have finely crushed gravel and are suitable for bicycling as well as hiking. A 1-mile self-guided nature trail has also recently been added. Encircling a marsh, interpretive signs help increase your understanding of the wetlands.

Drinking water, restrooms, play equipment, fishing in the ponds, picnic sites, and reservable shelters are available.

Des Plaines River Trail (DPRT) Southern Section

The southern section of the Lake County Forest Preserves' DPRT winds its way mostly through four adjoining forest preserves. Heading south the 8.75-mile trail starts up again at Rockland Road east of downtown Libertyville. The surface is crushed gravel. No public parking at the trailhead is available. The best place to leave your car is in the Old School Forest Preserve parking area near the northern trailhead or at the Half Day Forest Preserve near the southern trailhead.

How to get there:

The DPRT is just north of the entrance to Old School Forest Preserve on St. Mary's Road between Routes 137 and 60. If you plan to start at the southern end, park in Half Day Preserve. Directions on how to get there are given below.

If you want to bike or hike the entire southern section cross over St. Mary's Road and head west about 1 mile through open prairie and some wooded areas. The trail currently ends at Rockland Road. Then retrace your steps back to Old School Preserve.

Old School Forest Preserve

In winter, this 380-acre preserve provides a

Des Plaines River Trail (Southern Section)

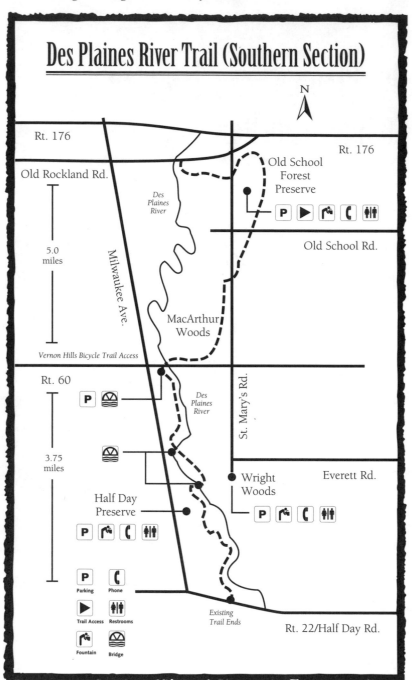

Old School Forest Preserve.

sledding hill on a manmade "mountain" and 5.7 miles of excellent cross country ski trails. Many warm weather activities are also available. A 1.6-mile auto road around the park has a lane for bike riding and is usually not crowded with cars. Shoreline fishing in the 12-acre lake will net you bass, crappie, and blue gill. Parking is available at several different sites throughout the preserve. I suggest you stop at the ranger station and pick up a colorful brochure with a map of Old School trails and facilities. Reservable shelters, restrooms, telephones, and drinking water are available. A lookout tower at the reservable Meadows shelter area offers a scenic view of a prairie overlooking the Des Plaines River valley.

In addition to the DPRT, 3.5 miles of hiking and biking trails through the woods and prairies are available. Three miles of crushed gravel multi-use trail meanders through the woods near the perimeter on the west, north, and south borders. Two-thirds of this trail is part of the DPRT. A 1.5-mile crushed gravel physical fitness trail with ten exercise stations runs through the deep woods in the center. A 1-mile gravel Lake Trail winds around Old School Lake in the northeast

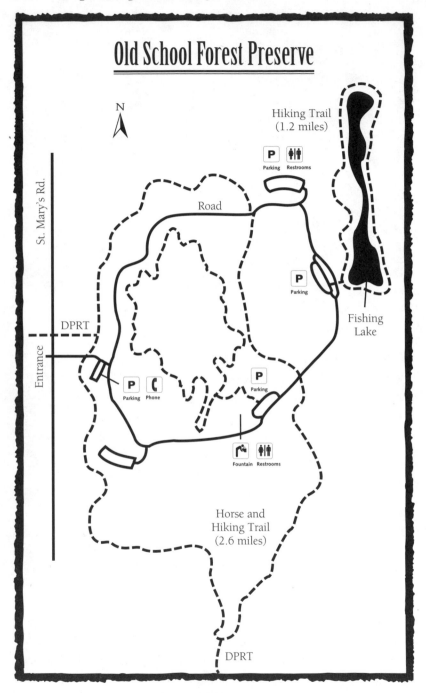

Old School Forest Preserve

N

Hiking Trail
(1.2 miles)

P Parking   Restrooms

Road

St. Mary's Rd.

DPRT

P Parking

Fishing
Lake

Entrance

P Parking   Phone

P Parking

Fountain   Restrooms

Horse and
Hiking Trail
(2.6 miles)

DPRT

corner of the preserve.

The DPRT leaves Old School Preserve as it crosses over Old School Road. The trail continues south by some homes and horse barns. A tunnel under St. Mary's Road leads you into MacArthur Woods.

MacArthur Woods Forest Preserve

The DPRT takes you through the east side of this beautiful 504-acre preserve of predominately maple woods. There is no development (other than the trail) in MacArthur Woods. Nothing but the trees. The Des Plaines River forms its western boundary. Please take special care of this land since it is protected as part of the Illinois Nature Preserves System. You'll traverse many curves on the trail. The trail was constructed so that trees would not have to be removed. Please go slowly.

The DPRT leaves MacArthur Woods at Route 60 and rejoins the river. An underpass takes you safely below the busy highway; that is, unless the spring showers have caused the river to flood thereby obstructing the underpass. In that case, either backtrack to from whence you came or very carefully cross Route 60 and walk right (west) about

Bridge crossing on the DPRT.

Lake County Forest Preserves

Wright Woods Forest Preserve.

100 yards to pick up the DPRT heading south. Be careful. Route 60 is a very busy highway. The safer place to cross Route 60 is at the stop light farther west. But we do not recommend doing so. Come back in the summer or fall for a longer bike ride or hike.

Just south of Route 60 and east of Milwaukee Avenue (Route 21) is a canoe launch area. Parking is available here. Many restaurants and stores are also nearby. The DPRT proceeds south through an open prairie. Watch for waterfowl in the marshes near the river. We passed two turtles on the trail during our last bike ride. One and one-half miles south of the canoe launch you will enter the privately owned Lloyd's Woods Nature Preserve. A bridge high over the Des Plaines has a great view with a small dam adding to an already picturesque setting. One quarter of a mile later you enter Wright Woods.

Wright Woods

At the time of writing, Wright had just re-opened after major renovation. As you proceed south on the DPRT past the bridge, you'll note three trails that head to the left. All three take you through the river

Wright Woods and Half Day Forest Preserves

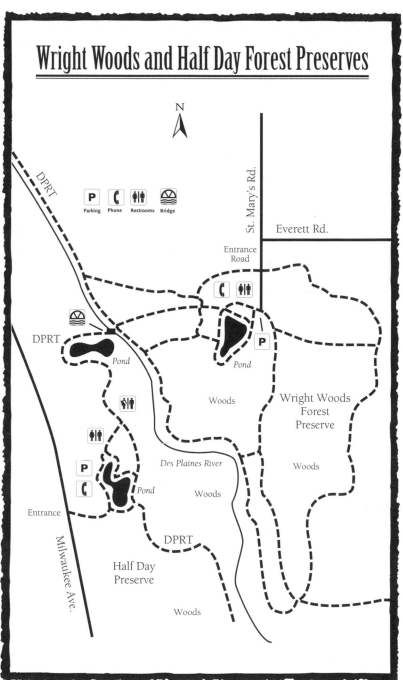

bottom land of Wright Woods. (See map). A new short trail accessible to the physically handicapped winds around a small pond next to the parking area. In the autumn, the sugar maple forest displays beautiful colors. Four and one-half miles of heavily wooded multi-use trails are available for bicycling, horseback riding, hiking, or cross country skiing. The trail surface is packed earth and crushed gravel.

This 327-acre preserve offers fishing, picnic areas, ranger station, and a new playground. Water, restrooms, and public telephones are available. The entrance to Wright Woods is at the intersection of St. Mary's and Everett Roads near Mettawa.

West of Wright Woods crossing over a bridge the DPRT enters Half Day Preserve.

Half Day Preserve
How to get there:

If you are starting at the DPRT south trailhead heading north, park in Half Day Preserve. The entrance is on Milwaukee Avenue (Route 21) 2 miles north of Route 22 and south of Route 60.

Lake County Forest Preserves

Half Day Forest Preserve.

This 201-acre preserve offers a mix of prairie, woods, and wetlands. Picnic sites, three reservable picnic shelters, play fields, a ranger station, restrooms, drinking water, a public telephone, and a 3-acre pond for fishing and ice skating are available.

The DPRT continues south of the Half Day Preserve to the southern trailhead at Old Half Day Road just north of Route 22. No convenient parking is available here. At the time of writing, the southern section of the DPRT is 8.75 miles. With a return trip to Old School Forest Preserve, you can have a 17.5-mile adventure through some very attractive natural areas.

Construction of a 3-mile extension north from Rockland Road to Route 137 is scheduled for the summer of 1994. There are plans to extend the DPRT to interconnect with the Buffalo Grove Trail System and the Cook County Des Plaines River trail that runs along the river through Potawatami Woods, and many other Cook County forest preserves and parks. The Cook County trail continues south to Touhy Avenue where it interconnects with the Indian Boundary Division Trail.

An open though unmarked trail in Ryerson Woods beginning at Lake Cook Road just west of Portwine Road will also be part of the DPRT, however, no parking is available there. If you'd like to hike it, you'll need to head south into Cook County.

How to get there:

Take Route 21 south of Lake Cook Road 1 mile to Dundee Road. Turn left (east) on Dundee for .2 mile to the Potawatami Woods Cook County Forest Preserve. Park in the first lot. The crushed gravel multiuse trail is to the west.

Take the trail to the right which leads north through a deeply wooded area. After about .9 mile you'll come to Lake Cook Road. Be careful crossing over. This is a very busy highway. The trail continues north into Ryerson Woods and ends at Greenbrier Lane in Riverwoods. When this portion of the DPRT is completed, we'll have opportunities for many more miles of hiking and biking through the forest preserves of both Lake and Cook Counties.

Vernon Hills Bikeways

Vernon Hills has an extensive 7-mile biking and hiking trail system that connects with the southern section of the Des Plaines River Trail at the Route 60 Canoe Launch.

How to get there:

Take Route 60 west of Route 21 in Vernon Hills. Turn right (north) on Lakeview Parkway .75 mile west of Route 21. Turn left into Century Park .5 mile north on Lakeview. Parking is also available at Deerpath Park south of Route 60. Deerpath Road is .25 mile west of Lakeview Parkway. Go south on Deerpath until you come to Cherokee Road. Turn left to Deerpath Park.

At the north end, in Century Park, the trail loops around Little Bear and Big Bear Lakes mostly through open fields with a brief interlude through the woods. Several bridges take you over water. Twenty exercise stations for joggers or walkers also surround the lake. The asphalt path system reaches out into neighborhoods of townhomes, single family residences, and apartments. Concessions, boat rental, public phones, restrooms,

The bikepath at Century Park in Vernon Hills.

playground equipment, and picnic tables are available. Children will also enjoy the large sledding hill.

There are plans to extend the west end of the path at Greenleaf Drive to head north along Butterfield Road to Libertyville. When completed the bikeway will connect with the western branch of the North Shore Path (see Section 5). After you finish exploring the 3.25 miles of paths around Century Park, take the trail south along Lakeview Parkway to Deerpath and Marimac Parks. There is a pedestrian button at the stoplight for crossing over Route 60. Turn right (west) at Phillip Road. The path left paralleling Lakeview Parkway takes you to the Des Plaines River Trail. More on that later. Three-quarters of a mile south of Route 60 is Deerpath Park. The bikeway wanders along tennis courts, a small lake, and the most playground equipment I've ever seen in a park. As you continue south, the path runs along the Seavey Creek to connect with Marimac Park.

An Arbortheater is currently under construction south of Marimac Park. On an 8-acre site, a natural amphitheater is being created. One-thousand trees will be planted. Ponds and waterfalls will be added.

The result will be a community garden and meeting place for plays, musical events, and other activities. The Arbortheater is expected to be completed in 1995.

Just as in the northern part of the bikeway, the path extends into and through residential neighborhoods ending at Route 45 and Deerpath Road. Plans are to extend it west and then south past the Village Hall to Sullivan Woods where a nature trail will be constructed. The bike path will be extended to a new commuter train station and also interconnect with the Buffalo Grove bike path system (see Section 15). This work is scheduled for completion in 1995.

As you head back north take the path right (east) along Lakeview Parkway to interconnect with the LCFPD's Des Plaines River Trail. The path loops around Freeway Drive and Bunker Court through an executive park. Continue on the parkway until you get to Milwaukee Avenue (Route 21). Turn left (north) then cross over Route 21 at the first stop light at the Hawthorn Woods shopping center. Continue east through the Rivertree Court shopping center. Turn left at the stop sign. A pathway along Route 60 connects with the DPRT at the boat launch area.

The Vernon Hills and the Buffalo Grove path systems provide excellent examples of community trails that offer safe transport for recreation, shopping, or commuting both internally as well as reaching out externally to interconnect with other trail systems. The Vernon Hills River Trail won the Local Project of the Year Award in 1992 from the Lake Branch of the American Public Works Association.

The Vernon Hills bike/park system is a good place for families with young children learning how to handle a two wheeler. There's no loose gravel to slip on and few sharp turns. The playground equipment provides a good break for parents and youngsters. A Vernon Hills Bikeways map is available at the Village Hall. Call 708-367-3700 for more information.

Ryerson Woods Conservation Area

Ryerson Woods, a 550-acre plant and wildlife sanctuary, is a crown jewel among Lake County's forest preserves and known as a mecca for spring bird watchers.

How to get there:

Located west of Deerfield on Riverwoods Road, the entrance is 1.8 miles south of Route 22 and 1.3 miles north of Deerfield Road. There is a 3-mile bike path on the east side of Riverwoods Road. Biking is not allowed on the trails at Ryerson. So, if you ride your bike, lockup at the rack near the Visitor's Center.

Two major Indian trails once intersected nearby; the Deer Trail connecting the Fox River with Lake Michigan and another trail that took early travelers from the Ohio Valley to Wisconsin and Lake Superior. In 1834, Daniel Wright, Lake County's first white resident, built a cabin near here. He was assisted by Chief Mettawa, a Potawatami Indian who lived nearby. His name carries on in the nearby community of Mettawa. A sawmill, general store, and river settlement called Half

Ryerson Woods Conservation Area

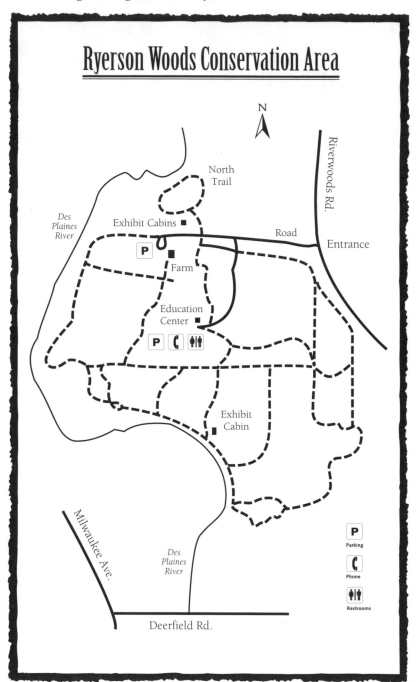

Mark Hurley, naturalist at Ryerson, with red-tailed hawk.

Lake County Forest Preserves

Day were soon built just north of Ryerson Woods on what is now Route 22.

Start your visit to Ryerson at the Visitor's Center near the parking lot. This was the Ryerson family's summer home until 1972. Much of the land was donated in the 1970s by Edward and Nora Ryerson of Inland Steel and other families. Take a few minutes and talk with the naturalist or receptionist in the center. Wander through the halls and see the beautiful nature pictures that fill the walls. Also there's an extensive library of books on wildlife, geology, botany, and other related sciences.

Free brochures for the north and south nature trails as well as an area map are available. The north trail guide describes the changes that have occurred in the area over the past few generations. Numbered posts identify the locations that relate to the descriptions in the guide. The south trail tree tour guide available in summer and fall, describes 15 different species of trees you will encounter. Again numbered posts identify them. In the spring, a wildflower trail brochure is available.

Cross country skiing is excellent here in the winter with the dense woods that provide some protection from the Chicago wind. A 4-inch snow base is required. In the spring, summer, and fall there is no better place to walk or hike. Park benches are strategically placed in several locations along the trails usually buried deep in the woods and often along the Des Plaines River. On a warm, sunny day, with the geese, ducks and herons on the river, the chipmunks and squirrels at play, the birds singing overhead, and an occasional deer wandering by, you become part of a tranquil scene that is hard to duplicate anywhere in the Midwest. Bring along a good book such as this guide and enjoy.

The shorter north trail is approximately .75 mile. Nearby are exhibit and program cabins as well as the Council Ring. Just south is a farm with beehives and domestic farm animals.

Five and three quarters miles of trails wind their way mostly through dense forest south and east of the Visitor's Center. Several bridges and boardwalks on the trails keep your feet dry and protect the vegetation. Markers and maps are available at each major trail

Lake County Forest Preserves

Cross country skiers on the trail.

Ryerson dam.

juncture to help you find your way through this beautiful place.

On the trail along the Des Plaines River you will find two cabins. The Smith river cabin contains a historical display. Farther down is the Ryerson river cabin and a dam.

Drinking water and restrooms are available. To help preserve the environment, picnic sites are not available. About half of Ryerson Woods is a dedicated nature preserve. Excellent programs are available year-round. The Ryerson Almanac is a free quarterly newsletter produced by the LCFPD. Call 708-948-7750 for more information.

Chicago Botanic Garden and the North Branch Bicycle Trail

We're cheating by including the Botanic Garden, because it is not actually located in Lake County. But it's so beautiful and interesting we couldn't avoid covering it a bit since it borders Lake County.

How to get there:

The main entrance is on County Line (Lake Cook Road) .4 mile east of U.S Route 41. Parking costs $4 per vehicle. Admission is free. From the Green Bay Trail at Braeside train station (see Section 1), you can bike or walk on the sidewalk on the north side of Lake Cook Road .6 mile to the main entrance where there is a stoplight for safe crossing. A separate bike pathway is planned to extend to the Green Bay Trail. The Garden can also be accessed from the south on bike or on foot through a walking-only entrance on Dundee Road just east of U.S. Route 41. If you visit the park on your bicycle, there are racks near the entrance to the gateway center. Bikes are not allowed on the garden trails.

Eight hundred thousand trees, shrubs, and plants are spread throughout the 300-acre

Chicago Botanic Garden

The Waterfall Garden.

Botanic Garden, which is owned by the Forest Preserve District of Cook County and managed by the Chicago Horticultural Society. Restoration of five different types of prairie communities is underway (fen, gravel hill, mesic, sand, and savanna). You'll enjoy 17 miles of walks and trails for touring the more than 20 different display gardens. Self-guided tour maps are available at the gateway center that describe the garden areas and walks ranging from .25 to 1.6 miles. Some examples are a 1.25-mile Japanese Garden Trail, a 1-mile Nature Trail through an oak-hickory forest, and a 1.5-mile Prairie Trail. Hours are from 8 a.m. to sunset, everyday of the year except Christmas.

The Botanic Garden is the trailhead for the 17-mile North Branch Bicycle Trail. Heading south from the Botanic Garden, the asphalt bike path travels through the Skokie Lagoons for 5.8 miles. South of Willow Road the trail passes through several Cook County forest preserves and roughly parallels the North Branch of the Chicago River for another 11.5 miles. On your way, you will pass through the Cook County communities of Glencoe, Winnetka, Northfield, Wilmette, Glenview (east of the Naval Air Station), and Niles. The off-road trail ends just after you enter Chicago at the intersection of Devon and Caldwell Avenues. There is an existing connection with the Chicago Bikeway System at Devon heading southeast. Water and restroom facilities are available along the way.

Call 708-835-5440 for more information about Chicago Botanic Garden. Many programs and activities are offered throughout the year. Call 708-366-9420 with questions concerning the North Branch Trail which is administered by the Forest Preserve District of Cook County.

Buffalo Grove Bike Path System

Just to the south of Vernon Hills is Buffalo Grove. Everything in the village seems new—from the post office to the shopping centers to the homes to the bike paths. The community has grown tremendously in the past few years. Because village planners had the foresight to include bike paths in development, Buffalo Grove has the most miles of designated bike paths of any site in Lake County. As of August 1993, there were 16.6 miles of off-street eight-foot wide asphalt paths, 16.3 miles of eight-foot wide concrete sidewalks, and 19.5 miles of planned paths spread throughout the 8.3 square mile village.

On all sides, the Buffalo Grove bike paths will interconnect with surrounding communities or LCFPD paths. On the southeast, a path is planned to interconnect with the Des Plaines River Trail (see Section 11) in 1995. To the north the Vernon Hills and Buffalo Grove path systems will interconnect at Prairie and Port Clinton Roads. To the west a bike path tunnel beneath Arlington Heights Road leads to the new Buffalo Creek Forest Preserve (see section 16). On the south, interconnection with a Wheeling bike path is planned.

Within the village you'll find bike paths practically everywhere—to the schools and shopping areas, through the residential neighborhoods and parks, along golf courses and prairie, and in wetlands. Many of the bike paths are yet to be interconnected. But when the additional 20 miles have been added, Buffalo Grove will have a very extensive path system. Local residents can bike to work, shopping centers, schools, churches, and recreational areas. "Bike Path" signs guide you on the trail. You can pick up an excellent map of the Buffalo Grove Bike Paths at the Village Center. The price is 25 cents.

We won't try to describe all the pathways through the neighborhoods here. We'll take a 12-mile round trip route through the community with a ride through wetlands and stops at the Village Green and the Buffalo Creek Forest Preserve.

How to get there:

You'll find many places to park throughout Buffalo Grove. To try the following route, we suggest using the parking lot at the Vernon Township Government offices building at the southwestern corner of Port Clinton and Prairie Roads on the far north side of Buffalo Grove.

Head west on the concrete sidewalk along Port Clinton Road just north of the parking lot. Follow the path south (left) as it intersects with Buffalo Grove Road. The Arboretum Golf Course lies on both sides of the path as you approach Half Day Road (Route 22). Take the bike underpass to avoid crossing this busy road. Continue south along Buffalo Grove Road to Aptakisic Road. Turn right to take a short loop (.8 mile) north through wetlands. Take the asphalt path right along the Com Ed right-of-way to ride through wetlands and marshes. After you return to and cross over Aptakisic Road, take the asphalt path west through a small prairie. The trail winds its way south through residential neighborhoods and Busch Knolls Park. Cross over Busch Road and proceed left (east) to Buffalo Grove Road. Turn right (south) on Buffalo Grove Road on the east side of the street. Proceed about .8 mile to the Rotary Village Green area. You'll find several restaurants among the shops to the east and south. Then continue south along Buffalo Grove Road to the Lake Cook intersection. Turn right (west) here on the north side of Lake Cook Road. Continue for

1.3 miles to Arlington Heights Road. Turn right (north) staying on the east side of the road. After another .3 mile, you'll come to an underpass that takes you beneath Arlington Heights Road to the Buffalo Creek Forest Preserve (see section 16). Hopefully, by the time you read this, the preserve trails will be completed.

After you leave the preserve, follow the asphalt trail right (east) where you will first go through a small prairie and then over Buffalo Creek. Take the path right with the bridge crossing over Buffalo Creek. The trail winds south and then east again along the Buffalo Grove Golf course. You'll come back to Lake Cook Road. Turn left (east) on the bike path back to Buffalo Grove Road Lane. Turn left (north) on Buffalo Grove Road.

On the far east side of Buffalo Grove, you can take a bike path around part of Chevy Chase Golf Course and then cross Milwaukee Avenue at the light at River Walk Parkway. Continue on the asphalt trail past the Des Plaines River. There are plans to interconnect with the Des Plaines River Trail here.

This gives you a sampling of the bike paths available in Buffalo Grove. The village has done and continues to do a fine job of providing bike paths within the community and reaching out for interconnection to the other trail systems. Call the Buffalo Grove Division of Planning Services at 708-459-2518 for more information.

Buffalo Creek Forest Preserve

Surrounded by the suburbs of Arlington Heights, Buffalo Grove, and Long Grove, the Buffalo Creek Forest Preserve is currently being developed with two totally different but complementary objectives. One is to restore 100 acres of farmland to prairie and savanna as it was 200 years ago. A reservoir was created several years ago when a dam was included for flood control. The lake is a magnet for waterfowl and other wildlife. There are several small islands in the reservoir. Nesting boxes will be installed on one of the islands to attract great blue heron. The other objective is to provide recreational opportunities for the human wildlife. At the time of writing, 4 miles of crushed gravel trails are being developed for hiking, biking, and cross country skiing with completion planned for 1994.

How to get there:

Buffalo Creek is located west of Arlington Heights Road and just north of Lake Cook Road. A parking lot is being installed on the north end of the preserve. Take Arlington Heights north

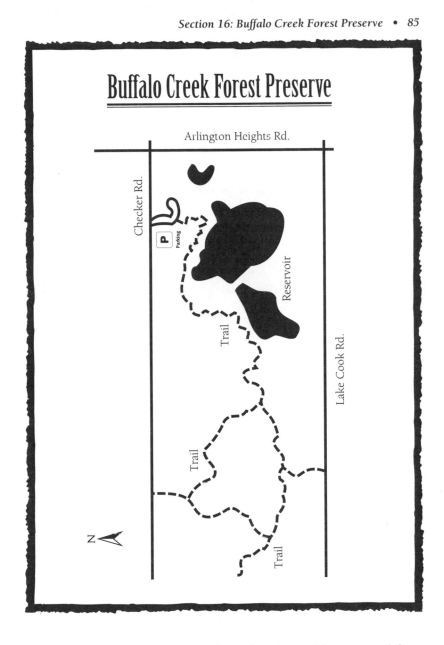

and turn left on Checker Road. The parking lot will be on your left.

Signs will be installed along the trails to describe the natural history of the area. Drinking water will be available. This 410-acre preserve is becoming an oasis of natural beauty right in the middle of suburbia.

Cuba Marsh

Cuba Marsh is a Lake County Forest Preserve that provides an opportunity to rough it a bit by hiking through undeveloped wetlands and prairie.

How to get there:

From Lake Cook Road take Ela Road 1.5 miles north to Cuba Road. Turn left (west) on Cuba for .5 mile. The entrance to Cuba Marsh is on the south side of the street. You'll need to park along Cuba Road. The Ela Marsh entrance is on Ela Road .5 mile south of Cuba Road. Again the only parking is along the road.

In the spring, I took an enjoyable hour hike (about 2.5 miles) through Cuba Marsh. Take the path to your right as you enter. The trail leads first through a beautiful tall oak forest then through a prairie with a large stand of pine trees on the left. After a mile or so, you'll enter a marsh area. The trail crosses a couple of small creeks and two small lakes and has some hills. The LCFPD is restoring the prairie and wetlands. My wife and I visited in summer and found the pathways at both Cuba and Ela Marshes too overgrown for a long walk. In late fall, we returned to the Cuba Marsh area. The trails had been mowed and the hiking was good. It's a peaceful, quiet place to walk.

Lakewood and the Lake County Museum

Located near Wauconda west of Mundelein and north of Lake Zurich is the county's largest preserve. Lakewood consists of 1,673 acres of rolling hills, several lakes and ponds, and dense woods.

How to get there:

The main entrance is just west of Fairfield Road on Route 176. Stop at the large map showing a layout of the preserve near the entrance.

Lakewood has the most extensive trail system of any Lake County Forest Preserve. Living up to its name, 9 miles of trails wind their way around the lakes and ponds and through the forest. The trails are mostly dirt and very wide.

Youth camping, picnic sites, drinking water, restrooms, ample parking facilities, five reservable shelters, fishing, and several play fields are available. Permits are required for shelter use. In winter, cross country skiing, sledding, ice skating, and snowmobiling trails are available.

If you intend to hike the 6.5 mile horse trail, take Ivanhoe Road inside the preserve to the

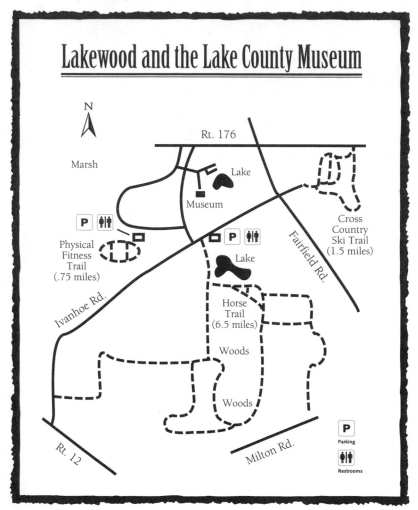

Lakewood and the Lake County Museum

gravel road with the sign identifying hiking and horse trails. When we visited, several horses and riders were on that trail. Nearby is an enjoyable .75-mile physical fitness trail which was dedicated in 1977 by former Olympic Decathlon champion, Bruce Jenner. The trail takes you up and down hills in the woods crossing over a small creek with 20 fitness stations if you're so inclined. You'll also find a 1.5-mile cross country ski trail located across Fairfield Road northeast of the main preserve area.

Lake County Forest Preserves

Lake County Museum.

After hiking the trails, you can warm up in winter or cool off in summer at the Lake County Museum. One of the state's largest, the museum is operated by the forest preserve district.

Exhibits trace the county's history through displays that interest children and adults. Visitors can enjoy relics reflecting Native American life and early settlers as well as horse-drawn carriages. A locally-discovered mastodon bone is a main attraction. The museum, which includes an education center, is a favorite stop for school children in spring and fall.

Hours are 11 a.m. to 4:30 p.m. Monday through Saturday and 1 to 4:30 p.m. Sundays. Admission is $1.50 for adults and 50 cents for students. Mondays are free. Call 708-526-7878 for more information.

Volo Bog State Natural Area

The 869-acre nature area containing the bog, marshes, woodlands, and prairies is just north of the Village of Volo.

How to get there:

Take U. S. Route 12 north of Volo. Turn left on Brandenburg Road. The entrance is 1.2 miles west of U. S. Route 12.

Volo Bog, one of the state's rarest ecosystems, provides habitat for some 25 Illinois-endangered plants as well as many bird species. This area offers a unique hiking experience providing visitors a glimpse of an Ice Age remnant. Due to its special nature, Volo Bog has been designated as a National Natural Landmark.

Stop first at the Visitor's Center which was converted from an old dairy barn. It is open 9 a.m. to 3 p.m. Thursday through Sunday. At other times, you can find helpful trail guides, maps and program listings outside. The preserve is open 8 a.m. to 4 p.m. daily, September through May, and until 8 p.m., June through August.

You'll find two hiking trails, a short Volo Bog Interpretive Trail and the longer Tamarack Trail, beginning near the Visitor's Center. The self-guiding .5-mile interpretive trail consisting of

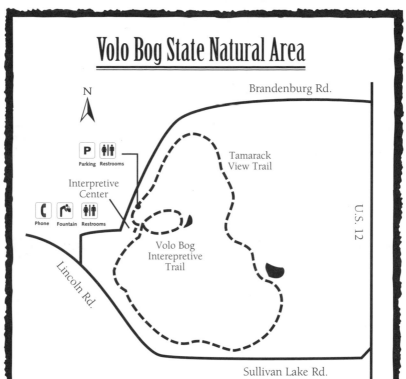

wooden dock sections, boardwalk, and a wood chip trail leads you to the bog. The 47.5-acre bog was originally a deep lake formed by the receding glacier that subsequently filled with vegetation. Sphagnum moss formed around the edges and eventually began to cover the entire lake. Cattails here attract red-winged blackbirds in spring.

The cattails give way to a moss-covered area filled with various ferns including cinnamon, marsh, royal, and sensitive fern, so named for its sensitivity to frost. Less noticeable are endangered wild orchids that can be found nowhere else in the county.

The trail guide admonishes hikers to stay on the boardwalk since the plants are rooted in a thin mat layer covering 50-feet of water and mucky bog. A viewing station overlooks the center of the bog where you can pause to listen to frogs singing or enjoy a duck swimming.

Volo Bog, which is on the migratory route for many waterfowl, is a

Volo Bog.

bird watcher's paradise. The best place to see the most birds is on the
2.75-mile Tamarack Trail. This fairly hilly trail meanders through oak
woods, open fields and prairie, and a marsh. Markers are placed at
each half mile. On a windy May afternoon, the sea of prairie grasses
rippled in the wind like ocean waves.

The trail earns its name from the endangered tamarack trees viewed
in the distant bog basin. Benches are available along the way. One particularly nice location is near the end of the hike looking down into
the bog through the trees. Also note near the end of the trail the pine ·
tree "meeting room" on the left. A narrow trail leads to a grove called
the Council of Pines where benches are arranged for programs and
presentations. The Tamarack Trail is open for cross country skiing in
the winter when there is snow base of at least six inches. Bicycling is
not allowed on the trails. A rack is available to lock up your bike.

The Volo Bog Natural Area is administered by the Illinois Department of Conservation. Visitors can enjoy programs and activities year-
round. A gift shop run by the Friends of Volo Bog is in the Visitor's
Center. A quarterly newsletter, The Bog Log, is available by subscrip-
tion. Restrooms, drinking water, telephone, and picnic areas are
provided. Bring your mosquito repellent during the summer. Call
815-344-1294 for more information.

Grant Woods Forest Preserve

Located east of the town of Fox Lake, Grant Woods is a 778-acre Lake County Forest Preserve of woods, prairie, and marshland.

How to get there:

Take U. S. Route 12 to Route 59 east of Fox Lake. Continue on Route 59 for 4 miles and then turn right (east) on Monaville Road. The entrance is just .1 mile east of Route 59.

Leave your car in the first parking area. The trailhead is just to the south of the restrooms. At the time of writing, there were no signs to direct the hiker. As you start walking on the 3.25 miles of crushed gravel trail, you will quickly come to an intersection. Either direction will take you south around a large marsh. See the map. The wide pathway is mostly flat and compact—good for biking as well as hiking.

You can enjoy panoramic views of the prairie and marsh surrounded on all sides by forest. Most of the trail in this area is along the marsh in open meadow or prairie land. After about 1 mile, you will come to another intersection. Here the two trails that took off in separate directions meet again.

The main trail continues south to Rollins Road

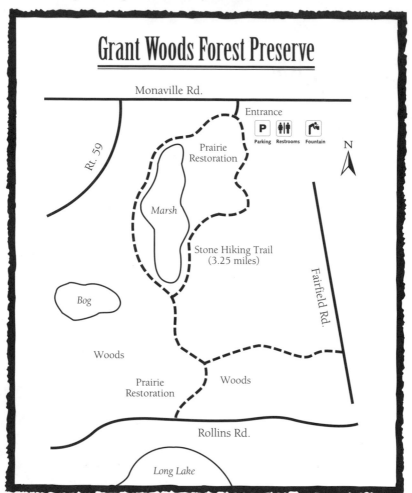

Grant Woods Forest Preserve

with a .6-mile side trail to the east that ends at Fairfield Road. This area is mostly deep woods. One spot on the side trail is particularly pleasant. During a spring visit, I came upon a sea of wildflowers growing under a stand of huge oak trees. Sitting on a bench gave me a feeling of being in a cathedral. This is a great spot to relax and enjoy the tranquil setting.

Grant Woods has drinking water, picnic tables, fields for games, reservable shelters, and restrooms as well as a few benches along the trails.

McDonald Woods Forest Preserve

$\mathbf{M}$cDonald Woods is a wonderful place to hike! You can wander through evergreen forests, wetlands, and meadows nestled in a valley of solitude.

How to get there:

The entrance to McDonald Woods is on Grass Lake Road .7 mile west of Route 45. Note the historic homes in the small village of Milburn as you turn onto Grass Lake Road.

You'll find 2 miles of crushed gravel trail for biking and hiking as well as a 1-mile wood chip trail. The crushed gravel trail loops around two large marsh ponds nestled in a valley. As you enter, walk through a prairie near a residential area and ball fields. In spring and summer, listen for the sounds of bobolinks, savanna sparrows, and meadowlarks singing in the grasses. Please be careful to stay on the trails since these birds nest on the ground and could easily be disturbed.

Walking down the hill past the grasses, you leave any signs of suburbia and approach a

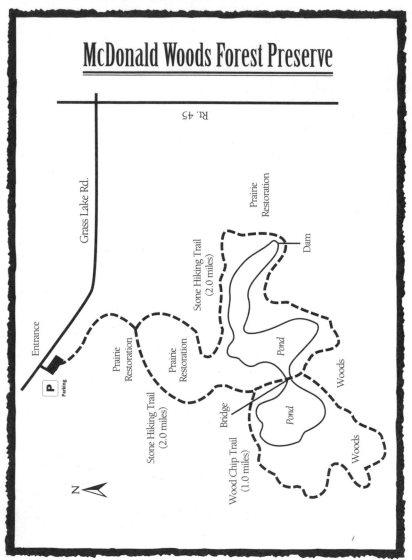

McDonald Woods Forest Preserve

tall pine forest on your left and a cattail marsh on the right. The trail
wanders initially through open meadows. A few benches offer places
to relax and enjoy the pines and marshes where ducks paddle lazily in
the foreground. Occasionally, on an early spring morning, you might
hear the maniacal call of the state-endangered pied-billed grebe from

Lake County Forest Preserves

Pond at McDonald Woods.

the wetlands. The preserve is listed in the Illinois Nature Areas Inventory because of the rare birds such as the grebe found here.

About halfway around the marsh, a wood chip trail to the left takes you up a fairly steep hill surrounded by evergreen and mixed forest. At this point you are well removed from the highway, so no vehicular sounds spoil the moment.

Here the trail winds through a stand of old pine forest and down into a ravine where you might see water striders skimming the surface. For a shorter hike, skip the wood chip trail up the hill. Instead walk across the bridge. Soon you will pass a gully bringing a small stream into the preserve.

Restroom facilities and drinking water will be available in summer 1994.

Chain O'Lakes State Park

The northwestern part of Lake County along with Lake Michigan certainly earn the county its name. This area has by far the largest concentration of lakes in Illinois. The Chain O'Lakes State Park borders three natural lakes—Grass, Marie, and Nippersink. The Fox River flows through the park before it empties into Grass Lake. The river connects seven other lakes that form the chain with over 6,400 acres of water and almost 500 miles of shoreline.

How to get there:

There are two entrances. To get to the main entrance from the south take Route 12 north of Fox Lake. Turn right onto Wilmot Road. Continue 2 miles to the park entrance. Coming from the north, take Route 173 and then head south on Wilmot. Be sure to get a map at the ranger station as you enter. The northern area of the park (Oak Point) can be accessed from an entrance on Route 173 just south of the Wisconsin border and west of Channel Lake. The Oak Point day use area has shelters, restrooms, picnic tables, and a canoe/boat launch

Chain O'Lakes State Park

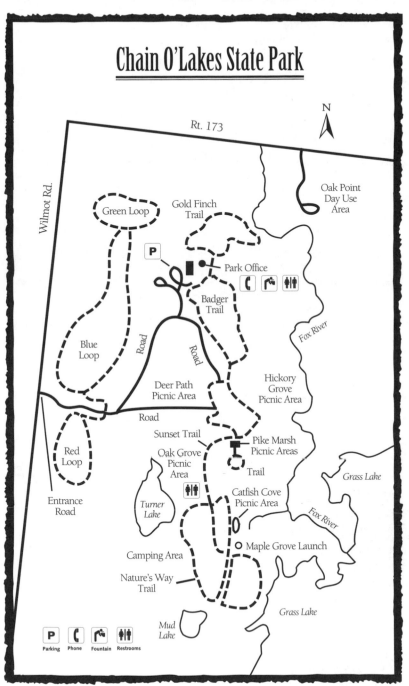

but no hiking trails.

Chain O'Lakes has one of the best trail systems in the area. You'll discover almost 16 miles of hiking trails and 5 miles of biking trails. In 1993, the Illinois Department of Conservation (IDOC) opened three new interconnecting crushed gravel hiking and biking trails. A fourth under construction is planned for completion in 1994. While you can pick up the trail at any of the picnic areas, I suggest driving to the north end of the park road and stopping at the park office. Here you'll find some interesting wildlife displays and a good view of the valley and the Fox River in the distance. The office is open Monday through Friday. The IDOC personnel are very helpful. Restrooms, drinking water, and bike racks are available.

The trailhead for the Gold Finch (Yellow) Trail is to the right (west) as you're leaving the park office. Each of the three new trails has a different color to identify the trail on marking posts along the pathway so you know where you're at—always a good idea! As you walk down the hill from the park office, note the prairie restoration underway. Throughout the park IDOC is restoring the tallgrass prairie that existed in this area 200 years ago. The Gold Finch Trail (1.75 miles) is a loop taking you through a medley of woodlands, open fields, marshes, and along the banks of the Fox River. The river is very wide here. You may see heron and other waterfowl as well as many wildflowers. The occasional bench or picnic table provides an opportunity to watch and contemplate.

The path to the right at the first trail intersection will take you back to complete the loop and to return to the park office. To continue on farther take a left (south) to connect with the Badger (White) Trail. You'll very quickly come to another trail intersection. Take a left onto the Badger Trail. Note the pine forest to your left. This area is mostly open meadow and prairie covering the rolling hills. The Badger Trail is also a loop. After about .75 mile there is yet another intersection. The path to the right will take you north continuing on the Badger Trail to the park office. The path to the left climbs a hill heading south and interconnects with the Sunset (Orange) Trail. Here you'll find a scenic view to the east with the Fox River and Grass Lake in the valley below. The Deer Path picnic area is just beyond the next trail intersection .1 mile farther south.

To continue south head left on the Sunset Trail. It winds its way through or near six picnic areas and ends at Catfish Cove near the Maple Grove Boat Launch. At the next trail intersection, the path to the left takes you first to the Hickory Grove area and then the Pike Marsh North picnic areas. The path to the right crosses over the park road at the Deer Path picnic area and continues south through the woods. You'll note a camera symbol sign along the trail with a short bark trail down to the marsh. A stick and hay thatched blind has been built by the marsh to watch and photograph the plentiful waterfowl. After about .5 mile, the trail again crosses over the park road at the Pike Marsh North picnic area. Most of these picnic areas have restrooms and drinking water as well as picnic tables. At Pike Marsh North there is a specially designed .25-mile trail accessible to the physically disabled user that runs through a woods. A platform overlooks the marsh.

Continue south on the Sunset Trail past the Pike Marsh south picnic area to a trail intersection. The right leg takes you across the park road where the trail ends at Honeysuckle Hollow campground. Beyond that lies 44-acre Turner Lake. The path to the left takes you farther south through the Oak Grove picnic area where you'll find playground equipment for the kids. Just south of the picnic area is the start of the Nature's Way Trail which is described below. The Sunset Trail ends at the Maple Grove Boat Launch. Concessions, a public telephone, restrooms, and a picnic area are nearby at Catfish Cove. Now it's time to retrace your path back north to the park office. As you enter the Badger Trail north of the Deer Path picnic area, take the pathway to the left to complete the 5 miles of new trails. You'll note the prairie restoration on your way back north.

The Cattail (Brown) Trail is under construction at the time of writing and will be open in 1994. This .7-mile path will run from the Sunset Trail west to the gatehouse near the main entrance. Along the way is an intersection with one of the equestrian trails (Red Loop) near the horse stable as described below.

The Nature's Way Trail mentioned above wanders through an oak and hickory forest, runs along a marsh and sedge meadow, and

Pike Marsh at Chain O'Lakes State Park.

overlooks Grass Lake with its cattail-lined shore. The surface of this 2.5-mile trail is wood chips and packed earth. There are some hills to climb and some nice views. Pick up a Nature's Way Trail Guide at the park office which describes interesting information at eight milestone stops.

Chain O'Lakes also offers 8 miles of equestrian trails on the west side of the park. The trails are open to hikers but bicyclers are not allowed. The northern trailhead is left (west) of the park office. A sign identifies the entrance. The mown grass trail leads to the east side of the Blue Loop Trail. (See map.) The path to the right leads north to the Green Loop, a 1.3-mile trail with some of the steepest hiking climbs in Lake County. Most of the trail is dirt with some gravel in spots. There are sharp curves at the top and bottom of the hills, so watch for horses. The Green Loop is through deep woods. The Blue Loop (4.7 miles) is a mixture of meadow and woods. To the south the Blue Loop leads to the Red Loop (2 miles).

Hikers can access the Red Loop Trail on foot from the Cattail Trail mentioned above. Also there is limited parking in the horse stable area. The Red Loop trailhead is across the road from the corral. Following the path to the left, you'll walk along the border of the forest and a prairie. It's very quiet and peaceful here with few highway sounds. As you proceed, the trail enters the woods with steeper hills. You'll enjoy the scenic views along the way.

The park trails are closed for hunting in November and December. In January, the trails re-open for cross country skiing as well as hiking. The park office serves as a warming station. Bike as well as boat/canoe rental is available April through mid-October at the concession area in Catfish Cove. Horse rental is available May through October at the horse corral. Call 708-587-5512 for more information.

Gander Mountain Forest Preserve

Nestled at the extreme northwest corner of Lake County bordering on Wisconsin and McHenry County stands the highest point in Lake County—Gander Mountain. This 290-acre preserve contains 2.5 miles of hiking trails.

How to get there:

Take Route 173 west to Wilmot Road. Turn right and proceed north approximately 1 mile. Look for a large Lake County Forest Preserve sign marking the entrance. Park right off the road by the barricade. There is no paved parking lot. Be sure not to block the gate.

Walk to your right after you pass the barricade. You'll note an opening at the end of the field with a dirt road. Follow that road approximately .5 mile. Turn left at the Y in the road to climb to the top of the mountain. You'll pass through an oak grove on the way. When you reach the top of the 957-foot elevation, you'll behold one of the prettiest vistas in the Chicago area. Hawks and turkey vultures soar above you. To the north is the Wilmot Winter Sports Area just

The view from Gander Mountain.

across the Wisconsin border. To the east lies Channel Lake. To the southeast is the Chain O'Lakes State Park and Grass Lake. To the west is farmland in McHenry County.

There are narrow pathways over to the Wilmot ski lift and down the mountain east. If you want a bit wider path, return down the hill to the Y intersection and walk left instead of back to your car. This will take you down a dirt road buried in the trees to the Fox River.

No restroom facilities and drinking water are available so bring your canteen as well as your hiking boots. During the growing season, the trail up the mountain may be overgrown at times if not recently mowed so you may want to wear long pants.

Greenway Interconnecting Trails

For the beginner hiker or biker, 1, 2, or 5 mile trails are sufficient to get exercise in an attractive outdoor setting surrounded by the beauties of nature. But over time many of us want to push on to the adventures of longer distances over different paths and trails. There is a growing interest by hikers and bikers to try new trails and pathways.

In Lake County, the rest of the Chicagoland area, and throughout the country, significant progress is being made to interconnect existing parks, forest preserves, and trails using old railroad or utility right-of-ways. The term greenways is being used to identify natural corridors of open land or water that will provide transport for people or wild animals while restoring or preserving the natural environment in that corridor. Often the trail is surrounded by neighborhoods, farms, or other developments. The greenway path usually provides hiking and biking opportunities for recreation or in some cases commuting to work. You may be able to use a greenways trail to visit a park or forest preserve on your bike rather than in your car. These linear park trails are typically much safer than the highways since contending with horses or bicycles is safer than dealing with cars, buses, and trucks. The Des Plaines River and Green Bay Trails as well as the North Shore Path described in Sections 1, 5, and 9, and 11 are examples of greenway trails.

The purpose of this section is to describe some of the activities underway to provide significantly more such trails in the near future within Lake County and to interconnect with trails originating in the surrounding counties of Cook and McHenry in Illinois, and Kenosha in Wisconsin. The Northeastern Illinois Planning Commission (NIPC) is partnering with the Chicago-based Openlands Project to help put in place an interconnected set of trails in the Chicagoland area that will cover 1,000 miles over the six-county Chicagoland area. There are already almost 350 miles of such greenways available. In five years it may be possible to make a 200-mile loop throughout the Chicagoland area to Wisconsin and back with most of the trip on dedicated off-road greenway trails. NIPC and Openlands Project, working with the six county forest preserve districts, local communities, and other organizations, have an exciting vision of interconnected trails in the Chicagoland area.

The Northeastern Illinois Regional Greenways Plan was released in May 1993 with this purpose—"The Greenways Plan creates a vision of an interconnected regionwide network of linear open spaces that will provide benefits to northeastern Illinois—environmental, recreational, economic, aesthetic, and even transportation via trails or waterways." Greenways may be waterways as well as paths on land. Greenways provide transport for not only humans but also for wildlife and plant seedlings. They preserve and protect water and air quality and animal life as well as provide recreational and self-propelled commuting. Greenway movements in Boston, New York, Seattle, and other metro areas have been very successful in linking together existing parks, forests, and trails. Given the high cost of land acquisition for parks and forests and the scarcity of available public funds, greenways are also proving to be the most cost effective means to provide access to open space. Old railroad right-of-ways, river flood plains, utility right-of-ways, and new community developments provide opportunities for the creation of new greenways.

The Northeastern Illinois Regional Greenways Plan encompasses Cook, DuPage, Kane, Lake, McHenry, and Will Counties. Greenway opportunities and priorities for development are laid out. The existing greenway network provides an excellent starting point including the major rivers (Chicago, Des Plaines, DuPage, and Fox), the Lake Michigan shoreline, old railroad routes (the Great Western Trail in DeKalb and Kane County, the North Shore Path in Lake County, the Illinois Prairie Path in Cook, DuPage, and Kane Counties, and the Virgil Gilman Trail in Kane County) and even old canals (The Illinois and Michigan Canal National Heritage Corridor).

Focusing on the Lake County portion, 180 miles of primary trails are envisioned with more greenways and trails in the central and western sections. Hooking these arteries up with local municipal trail systems such as Vernon Hills' or Buffalo Grove's paths will provide an exciting and enjoyable network of trails criss-crossing Lake County and interconnecting with the surrounding counties.

The Northeastern Illinois Greenways Plan identified the following priorities in Lake County:

1) Creation of greenways for the three Chicago River tributaries in southeastern Lake County (Skokie River, Middle Fork, and West Fork).

2) Completion of the Des Plaines River Trail corridor.

3) Creation of the Fox River Greenway.

4) Completion of the Greenbay Trail from Highland Park to Fort Sheridan.

5) Creation of greenways on undeveloped areas of the Lake Michigan shoreline such as Fort Sheridan.

6) Extension of the west branch of the North Shore Path from Lake Bluff to Libertyville interconnecting with the Des Plaines River Trail and connection of the northern portion with the Illinois Beach State Park trail system.

7) Extension of the west leg of the North Shore Path to Wauconda. Establishment of other east-west linkages to provide more access to and from western Lake County with a West Lake County Loop Trail.

Other potential Lake County greenways have been identified. Grayslake, Gurnee, Highland Park, and Libertyville plan to either establish new or expand existing trail systems.

NIPC and the Openlands Project provide an excellent vision and framework but community and county governments, regional agencies and organizations, federal and state governments, and private sector corporations, landowners, and interested individuals must play a role in turning the plan into reality. Voice your areas of interest if you'd like to be involved in making the Chicagoland Greenways network happen. For more information call NIPC at 312-454-0400 and/or Openlands Project at 312-427-4256.

Beyond Chicagoland

In the introduction to his book, Greenways for America, Charles E. Little describes the greenway initiatives as a "remarkable citizen-led movement to get us out of our cars and into the landscape—on paths and trails through corridors of green that can link city to country and people to nature from one end of America to the other." Little traces the origins of greenways back to architects such as Fredrich Law Olmsted, creator of Central Park in New York City. He describes examples both new and old from the Big Sur in California to the Illinois and Michigan Canal National Heritage Corridor to the Hudson River Valley Greenway in New York. The book is an excellent primer for those interested in furthering the development and interconnection of greenways.

The National Park Service, the American Hiking Society, and a coalition of individuals and many trail support organizations are partnering in an effort called "Trails for All Americans—The National Trails Agenda Project." This effort began in 1988 when the President's Commission on American Outdoors recommended the development of a nationwide network of hiking and jogging trails, bikeways, and bridle paths, similar to the U.S. Interstate Highway System. It is envisioned that there would be major backbone interstate trails with state, county, and local community trails and interconnecting paths. The hope is that most Americans would live within 15 minutes of a path that could access this national network.

The National Park Service has identified four categories of trails: *National Scenic Trails*—"continuous extended routes of outdoor recreation within protected corridors"; *National Historic Trails*— "recognize past routes of exploration, migration, and military action. These are not necessarily continuous, but feature outstanding high potential trail sites and segments"; *National Recreation Trails*— "existing Federal, State, or local trails recognized as components of the National Trails System." (As of the 1992-93 Edition of *The Complete Guide to America's National Parks,* 780 trails totaling 9,000 miles had been registered.); *Side and Connecting Trails* "provide additional access to components of the National Trails System."

The eight National Scenic and nine Historic Trails provide the major backbone network. Some examples are described below:

• The Appalachian National Scenic Trail—a completed 2,144 mile trail through the Appalachian Mountains from Katahdin, Maine to Springer Mountain, Georgia.

• The Ice Age National Scenic Trail—follows the path of glacier activity in Wisconsin. Four hundred fifty of 1,000 miles are completed.

• The Trail of Tears National Historic Trail—follows the two routes used to move 16,000 Cherokee Indians from Tennessee to Oklahoma, in 1838 and 1839. The water route covers 1,226 miles on the Tennessee, Ohio, Mississippi, and Arkansas Rivers. The 826-mile land route starts in Tennessee, crosses through Kentucky, the southern tip of Illinois, and then Missouri before the sad saga reaches its end in Oklahoma. Development of the entire trail plan has not yet been completed.

While no existing National Scenic or Historic Trail runs through Lake County, there has been a local effort to establish a Tecumseh Trail which has been envisioned to run from the Canadian border to southern Florida. See Section 25.

Proposed Tecumseh Trail

In 1971, Lee Nading conceived the idea of a 2,800-mile hiking trail from the northern boundary of Minnesota to Florida and the Gulf of Mexico. In 1980, the Tecumseh Trail Project was initiated to coordinate the development. The plan envisioned the first border to border trail in the Midwest crossing nine states from Ontario, Canada to the Gulf of Mexico. Linkage to the Appalachian Trail in northern Georgia and the Florida trail would be established.

Originally the Tecumseh Trail was conceived to be a wilderness pathway for hiking only. Later efforts expanded the concept to a multi use trail for equestrians, bicyclists, and others. In the late 1980s, the study route was reviewed and deemed to be feasible despite ongoing commercial, residential, and highway development.

The Illinois Trailriders Association describes the trail namesake as follows: "Tecumseh was a chief of the North American Indian tribe of the Shawnees. He was a gifted orator and magnanimous military leader and the determined advocate of an Indian confederacy

Tecumseh Trail

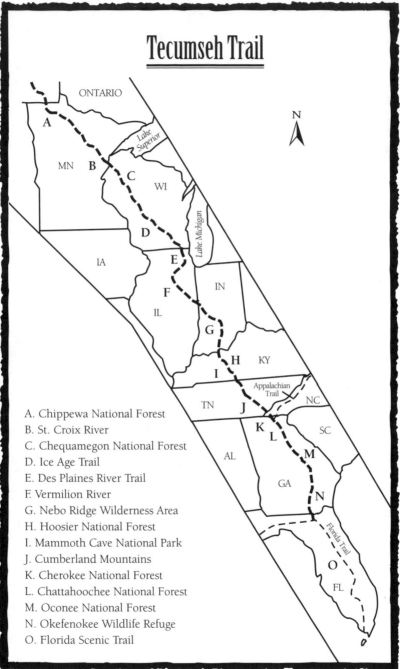

A. Chippewa National Forest
B. St. Croix River
C. Chequamegon National Forest
D. Ice Age Trail
E. Des Plaines River Trail
F. Vermilion River
G. Nebo Ridge Wilderness Area
H. Hoosier National Forest
I. Mammoth Cave National Park
J. Cumberland Mountains
K. Cherokee National Forest
L. Chattahoochee National Forest
M. Oconee National Forest
N. Okefenokee Wildlife Refuge
O. Florida Scenic Trail

in the late 18th and early 19th centuries. He urged intertribal alliance amongst the Indians and preservation of their culture. As the white man advanced upon their territory, he tried to save for his people the ancient lands. Tecumseh's cause failed, but his vision and zeal put him among the great leaders of primitive peoples who have tried to protect their homelands and their culture against the inexorable advance of civilization."

The map shows the proposed trail route and some of the existing forests, parks, and trails that would be included in the 2,800-mile route. In Lake County, the Des Plaines River Trail will be part of the Tecumseh Trail. Many miles of trail already exist in the national forests, parks, and other locations that will become a part of the Tecumseh Trail. But these individual sites are not interconnected. The majority of the route is still in the conceptual stage.

Most recently Ruby Holmquist, President of the Illinois Trailriders, has fostered interest in the Tecumseh Trail. Her involvement in national trails conferences and the Illinois Trailriders support have kept the concept alive. Equestrian groups in Georgia are becoming interested. However, unless other organizations and individuals get involved, the Tecumseh Trail will not become a reality. Call 708-395-0159 for more information.

Appendices

Nearby Attractions

401 N. Riverside Drive, Suite 3
Gurnee, IL 60031
1-800-525-3669

Participants with the Lake County, Illinois Convention &
Visitors Bureau are listed on the following pages 115 to 116.

Accommodations:

Adventure Inns
3732 Grand Avenue, Gurnee 60031
(708) 623-7777   (800) 373-5245

American Inn Motel
39018 Sheridan Road, Zion 60099
(708) 746-2095

Best Western Regency Inn
350 Route 173, Antioch 60002
(708) 395-3606   (800) 528-1234

Comfort Inn
6080 Gurnee Mills Circle E., Gurnee
60031
(708) 855-8866   (800) 221-2222

Comfort Inn
3031 Belvidere Road, Waukegan 60085
(708) 623-1400   (800) 228-5150

Courtyard by Marriott
1505 County Line Road, Highland Park
60035
(708) 831-3338   (800) 321-2211

Courtyard by Marriott
505 Milwaukee Avenue, Lincolnshire
60069
(708) 634-9555   (800) 321-2211

Courtyard by Marriott
800 Lakehurst Road, Waukegan 60085
(708) 689-8000   (800) 321-2211

Fairfield Inn
6090 Gurnee Mills Circle E., Gurnee
60031
(708) 855-8868   (800) 228-2800

Hampton Inn
5550 Grand Avenue, Gurnee 60031
(708) 662-1100   (800) HAMPTON

Hawthorn Suites
10 Westminster Way, Lincolnshire 60069
(708) 945-9300   (800) 527-1133

Hilton Garden Inn
900 W. Lake Cook Road,
Buffalo Grove 60089
(708) 215-8883   (800) HILTONS

Holiday Inn
6161 Grand Avenue, Gurnee 60031
(708) 336-6300   (800) HOLIDAY

Hyatt
1750 Lake Cook Road, Deerfield 60015
(708) 945-3400   (800) 228-9000

Marriott Suites
Two Parkway North, Deerfield 60015
(708) 405-9666   (800) 228-9290

Marriott's Lincolnshire Resort
Ten Marriott Drive, Lincolnshire 60069
(708) 634-0100   (800) 228-9290

Ramada Inn
200 N. Green Bay Road, Waukegan 60085
(708) 244-2400   (800) 2 RAMADA

Red Carpet Inn
3207 Buckley Road, North Chicago 60064
(708) 689-9400   (800) 251-1962

Round Robin Guesthouse
Bed & Breakfast Inn
231 E. Maple Avenue, Mundelein 60060
(708) 566-7664

Super 8
630 N. Green Bay Road, Waukegan 60085
(708) 249-2388   (800) 843-1991

Thriftlodge
222 Grand Avenue, Waukegan 60085
(708) 244-8950   (800) 525-9055

Attractions:

Arlington In Waukegan Off Track
Wagering Parlour
630 S. Green Bay Road, Waukegan 60085
(708) 336-1400

Cuneo Museum and Gardens
1350 N. Milwaukee Avenue, Vernon Hills
60061
(708) 362-2025

David Adler Cultural Center
1700 N. Milwaukee Avenue, Libertyville
60048
(708) 367-0707

Fun Harbour
651 Lakehurst Road, Waukegan 60085
(708) 578-5400

Gold Pyramid House
37921 Dilley's Road, Wadsworth 60083
(708) 662-6666

Lake County Fairgrounds
P.O. Box 216 (Route 45 & IL 120),
Grayslake 60030
(708) 223-2204

Lake County Museum
27277 Forest Preserve Road, Wauconda
60084
(708) 526-7878

Lambs Farm
P.O. Box 520 (Route 176 & I-94),
Libertyville 60048
(708) 362-4636   (800) 52-LAMBS

Marytown/St. Maximilian Kolbe Shrine
1600 West Park Avenue, Libertyville 60048
(708) 367-7800

The Power House
100 Shiloh Blvd., Zion 60099
(708) 746-7080

Six Flags Great America
P.O. Box 1776 (I-94 & Route 132 East),
Gurnee 60031
(708) 249-1776

Tempel Farms
17000 Wadsworth Road, Wadsworth
60083
(708) 244-5330

Wauconda Orchards
1201 Gossell Road, Wauconda 60084
(708) 526-8553   (800) 36-APPLE

Waukegan Symphony Orchestra
& Concert Chorus
39 Jack Benny Drive, Waukegan 60087
(708) 244-1660

Shopping:

Gurnee Mills Mall (708) 263-7500
(800) YES SHOP
6170 W. Grand Ave. (I-94 & Rte.132 W),
Gurnee 60031

Holiday Shoppe & Studio
(708) 662-1212
5101 W. Washington Street, Gurnee 60031

Long Grove Historical Village
(708) 634-0888
307 Old McHenry Road (Rtes. 53 & 83),
Long Grove 60047

MainStreet Libertyville
(708) 680-0336
507 N. Milwaukee Avenue,
Libertyville 60048

Did you ever see a Carbon Cycle?

Visit the *Chemical Energy Display*

Learn about energy at this hands-on museum where kids learn by doing. There's a miniature Old Faithful. A bike they can ride to generate electricity. The Power House was developed to help us all understand the important energy issues facing us.

The Power House
**Open Monday through Saturday, 10-5.
Free admission. Gift Shop. Cafeteria.
Call (708) 746-7080.**

Just off the *Zion Park District Bike Trail* on Shiloh Blvd. Leave the Trail at Zion's Northwestern RR commuter station, and ride about 3/4 mile east. We're right on the lake front, near the nuclear generating station.

Rest for the weary

- Historic adoration chapel open 6 am - 11 pm daily
- Giftshop/bookstore open 9:30 am - 5 pm, Mon - Sat
- Rosary/confessions 7 pm daily
- Restrooms/picnic tables/benches
- St. Francis fountain/stations of cross
- Right off North Shore path west branch: Rt. 176 at Libertyville/Mundelein border

THE FRIARS WELCOME
EVERYONE OF ALL FAITHS
TO STOP BY!

MARYTOWN/ST. MAXIMILIAN KOLBE SHRINE
Rt. 176 (1600 W. Park Ave.), Libertyville, Illinois 60048 • 708-367-7800

The Annual
LAKE COUNTY RACES
April's Premier Running Event

30 Minutes North of Chicago

Marathon

Half Marathon

10K Run

5 Person Marathon Relays

3.5 Mile Fun Run and Walk

For Application, send a self-addressed stamped envelope to: Lake County Races, 454 Central Ave. #201, Highland Park, IL 60035 Or call: 708/266-RACE

Calendar of Events

Each event is shown under the month scheduled in 1994. Most events are held annually in same month. Call to get specific information.

January

Chili Open Golf Tournament
Scout Klondike Derby
Lake County Forest Preserves   708-367-6640

Winterfest
Volo Bog   815-344-1294

February

Chili Open Golf Tournament
Groundhog Day
Lake County Forest Preserves   708-367-6640

March

Annual Midwest Indoor Triathlon
Center Club Tri-Classic Series
Libertyville   708-527-3672

Maple Syruping
Lake County Forest Preserves   708-367-6640

St. Patrick's Day Invitational—25M Ride
Wheeling Wheelmen
Wauconda Orchards   708-367-6472

April

Brae Loch Golf Course—Opens for play
Chandler's Boat & Bait, Inc.—Season Opens
Countryside Golf Course—Opens for play
Sheep Shearing
Lake County Forest Preserves   708-367-6640

Earth Day Events at Heller
Interpretive Center and Nature Park   708-433-6901

Ecofest
Volo Bog   815-344-1294

Lake County Races—Marathon, Half Marathon,
10K, Relays and Funwalk
Zion to Highland Park   708-266-RACE

May

Bike Open House
Evanston Bike Club   708-866-7743

Des Plaines River Canoe Marathon
Fox River Recreation Area—Season Opens
International Museum Day
Smith Symposium
Lake County Forest Preserves   708-367-6640

"Running with Angels"-2M/10K Runs
Becky Bell Family Fun Run
Lake Forest   312-786-0460

June

Annual St. Mary's—2/5M Runs
"Run for Nicole"
Buffalo Grove   708-541-0432

Bicycle Club of Lake County Ramble
36/60/100M
Wauconda   708-367-3341

Civil War Days
Firefighter Awareness Day
National Trails Day
Senior Day Celebration
Lake County Forest Preserves   708-367-6640

Motorcycle Ride In (First Week of June)
Illinois Beach State Park   708-662-4811

Ravinia Concerts (June-September)
Highland Park   312-RAVINIA

July

Budweiser Jet-Ski Tour (last week of July)
Nostalgia Days (Mid-July)
Illinois Beach State Park   708-662-4811

Deerfield Family Days (July 4)—
10K Run/5K Walk
Deerfield   708-945-2215

Lake County Fair (Late July)
Grayslake   708-223-2204

Summer Concert
Volo Bog   815-344-1294

August

Blue Grass Festival
Model Boat Races
Lambs Farm, Libertyville   708-362-4636

Gurnee Days Pepsi Race—2M/10K Runs
Gurnee   708-623-7788

National MS Society—Bike and Hike "94
Des Plaines River Trail   312-922-NMSS

September

Bagpipes & Bonfires
Lake Forest Open Lands   708-234-3880

Condell Distance Classic—10K Run/5K Walk
Condell Medical Center
Libertyville   708-362-2905

Fall Fishing Derby
Farm Heritage Tractor & Steam Show
Lake County Forest Preserves   708-367-6640

Harmon Hundred Mile Ride
Wheeling Wheelmen
Wauconda Orchards   708-367-6472

Illinois Prairie Week
Lake Forest Open Lands   708-234-3880

Jubilee Days (Labor Day)—2M/10K Runs
Zion   708-746-5500

Miles for Monte—5K Run/5K Walk/1M Family
Funwalk-Les Turner ALS Foundation
Lincolnshire   708-679-3311

MS Great Lake Getaway Bike Tour—150K Ride
National Multiple Sclerosis Society
Libertyville to Lake Geneva   312-922-NMSS

North Shore Century Invitational—
25/50/100M Rides
Evanston Bike Club   708-866-7743

Run for the Health of It—10K Run
Sunset Foods/Highland Park Hospital
Highland Park   708-432-2884

September Stampede—10K Run
Buffalo Grove   708-459-5700

October

Autumn Fest
Autumn Hayrides
Make A Difference Day
Ryerson Woods
Sterling Lake Fishing Derby
Lake County Forest Preserves   708-367-6640

Lambs Farm Haunted Train and Ghostwalk
Libertyville   708-362-4636

Lake County Family YMCA Annual Airfest
Waukegan Regional Airport   708-360-YMCA

Red Ribbon Classic—5K Run
Libertyville   708-367-3100

Windy City Sports Chili Bike Ride—
15/35/65/100M Rides
Zion Benton High School   312-421-6827

Witches Walk
Lake Forest Open Lands   708-234-3880

November

Corporate Championship Race 5K (Team Event)
Condell Medical Center
Center Club, Libertyville   708-816-6100

Turkey Open Golf Tournament
Lake County Forest Preserves   708-357-6640

December

Volunteer Recognition Dinner
Lake County Forest Preserves   708-367-6640

Other regularly scheduled events:

Lake County Museum Exhibits   708-948-7750

Monday Movers
Ryerson Woods Nature Exhibits
Volunteer Conservation Workdays
Lake County Forest Preserves   708-367-6640

Have Lunch on Windy City Sports!

CHILI RIDE

15 35 65

4th Annual Bike Rally

Join us for a beautiful fall bicycle ride
and a **FREE** lunch of piping hot chili on

Sunday, October 2.

Distances are **15, 35, 65** & **100** miles. The routes are
primarily flat, but there are some rolling hills and
a few strong climbs. The ride starts and finishes at
Zion-Benton High School, 3901 21st Street.

For more information please call:

312-421-6827

Organizations

Bicycle Clubs

Bicycle Club of Lake County   708-450-8294
Box 521
Libertyville, IL., 60048

Chicagoland Bicycle Federation   312-42 PEDAL
343 S. Dearborn, Suite 1017
Chicago, IL., 60604

Evanston Bike Club   708-866-7743
P. O. Box 1981
Evanston, IL., 60204

Recreation for Individuals Dedicated 800-458-2358
to the Environment (RIDE)   or 312-853-2820
Suite 1700, 208 S. LaSalle
Chicago, IL., 60604

Wheeling Wheelmen   708-367-6472
P. O. Box 581-D
Wheeling, IL., 60097

Environmental

Friends of Ryerson Woods   708-948-7750
Ryerson Conservation Area
21950 North Riverwoods Road
Deerfield, IL., 60015

Friends of Heller   708-433-6901
Heller Nature Center
636 Ridge Road
Highland Park, IL., 60035

Illinois Dunesland Preservation Society   708-746-1090
P. O. Box 466
Zion, IL., 60099

Lake Forest Open Lands Association   708-234-3880
560 North Oakwood Avenue
Lake Forest, IL, 60045 *

Nature Conservancy, Illinois Field Office   312-346-8166
79 West Monroe
Chicago, IL., 60603

The Friends of Volo Bog   815-344-1294
28478 West Brandenburg Road
Ingleside, IL., 60041

Hiking and Walking

American Hiking Society   703-385-3252
P. O. Box 20160,
Washington, D. C., 20041

Gurnee Mills Milers   708-263-7500
6170 West Grand Avenue
Gurnee, IL., 60031

Hawthorn Hikers   708-573-1300
Hawthorn Center
Townline Road and Milwaukee Avenue
Vernon Hills, IL., 60061

Other

Illinois Trailriders (A statewide equestrian group)   708-395-0159
P. O. Box 96
Wadsworth, IL., 60083

Lake County Museum Association   708-526-7878
Lakewood Forest Preserve
27277 Forest Preserve Drive
Wauconda, IL., 60084

Riverwoods Nature Photographic Society   708-948-7750
Ryerson Conservation Area
21950 North Riverwoods Road
Deerfield, IL., 60015

*Lake Forest Open Lands Association is a private, not-for-profit land preservation group founded in 1967 to protect open space in Lake Forest and promote educational and scientific understanding as well as recreational enjoyment for its membership. Open Lands currently owns and manages over 250 acres of rare virgin prairie, oak savanna, and wetlands with 8 miles of trails throughout. The association depends upon members for operating costs, however day passes ($1.00) are available to non-members, and these are easily acquired by calling the Lake Forest Open Lands office at 234-3880.

Bibliography

Articles

"Des Plaines River in forefront of angler's surprising gains". *Chicago Tribune*, Husar, John. May 9, 1993.

"Happy Trails". *Chicago Tribune*, Husar, John. July 14, 1993.

" 'Happy trails' part of County Forest Preserve". *Pioneer Press Newspapers*. Teague, Jim Jr. May 13, 1993.

"One lake, two worlds—Visitors can double their fun at Illinois Beach State Park". *Chicago Tribune*. Carlstone, Linda Mae. September 19, 1993.

"Prairies vital to ecosystem". *Pioneer Press Newspapers*. DeVore, Sheryl. September 17, 1993.

"Small prairie setting its roots with human touch". *Chicago Tribune*. Swanson, Stevenson. September 26, 1993.

Books

The Complete Guide to America's National Parks. National Park Foundation. 1992–93 Edition.

Country Walks Near Chicago. Fisher, Alan. Rambler Books. 1987.

Greenways for America. Little, Charles E. Johns Hopkins University Press. 1990.

Lake County, Illinois, This Land of Lakes and Rivers, An Illustrated History. Mullery, Virginia. Windsor Publications. 1989.

Portrait of the Midwest. Waitley, Douglas. Abelard-Schuman. 1963.

Other Publications

Horizons. Quarterly newsletter of the Lake County Forest Preserve District.

Ryerson Almanac. Quarterly newsletter of Ryerson Conservation Area of the Lake County Forest Preserve District.

The Northeastern Illinois Regional Greenways Plan. Developed by the Northeastern Illinois Planning Commission and Openlands Project. May, 1993.

Trails for all Americans—The Report of the National Trails Agenda Project. Submitted by American Trails to the National Park Service. Summer, 1990.

ORLAND PARK PUBLIC LIBRARY

Comments from Our Customers

Your comments related to this guidebook are very much appreciated for our use in improving future issues.

_____

_____

_____

_____

We are also considering publishing other hiking/biking guidebooks. Would you be interested in the following?

	Level of Interest		
	High	Medium	Low
• Hiking in Indiana's Parks and Forests	☐	☐	☐
• Hiking Made Easy in the Great Smoky Mountain National Park	☐	☐	☐
• Hiking and Biking in Door County, Wisconsin	☐	☐	☐
• Hiking and Biking in DuPage County, Illinois	☐	☐	☐
• Hiking and Biking in Cook County, Illinois	☐	☐	☐
• Hiking and Biking in Kane and McHenry Counties, Illinois	☐	☐	☐
• Exploring Dinosaur National Monument (Children's Book)	☐	☐	☐

We will be happy to include you on our mailing list to announce any upcoming products. Obviously, there's no obligation.

Name _____

Address _____

City, State, Zip Code _____

Thanks for your input.

Order Form

Send _____ copy/copies of *Hiking & Biking in Lake County, Illinois* to the following address:

Name _____

Address _____

City, State, Zip Code _____

Please enclose a personal check for the total amount made payable to Roots & Wings, P.O. Box 167, Lake Forest, Illinois, 60045. Thank you for your order!

_____ books @ $10.95   = _____

Illinois Residents Add
Sales Tax @ 6.5% (or   = _____
$.71/book)

Shipping and Handling   = __$1.95__

Total   = _____

Also you may buy additional copies of the guidebook at bookstores, bicycle shops, sporting goods stores as well as other merchants throughout the Chicagoland area.